CULTURAL STORY OF AN AMERICAN CITY

CLEVELAND

PART III
UNDER THE SHADOW OF A CIVIL WAR AND RECONSTRUCTION
1850-1877

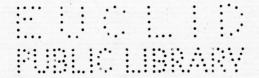

Elbert Jay Benton

The Publication of this study is made possible by the
Philip L. Cobb Memorial Fund

WESTERN RESERVE HISTORICAL SOCIETY
CLEVELAND, 1946

Publications of the Western Reserve
Historical Society

New Series   Number III

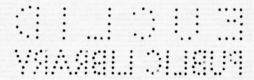

CONTENTS

CONTENTS — *Continued*

CULTURAL STORY OF AN AMERICAN CITY

PART III

UNDER THE SHADOW OF A CIVIL WAR AND RECONSTRUCTION

1850-1877

I. THE PASSING OF CANAL DAYS

CANAL DAYS—Part II of the Cultural History of Cleveland was devoted to the Canal Days, 1825-1850. The Ohio canals meant new ways of life for Clevelanders. The inhabitants of those times saw Cleveland grow from a village, among the least of those of the Western Reserve, to the metropolitan city of northern Ohio; they were parties to the rise of churches, newspapers, schools and the fine arts. The establishment of a library, a natural history museum, two medical schools and a university seemed to constitute a grand climax in the rapid development of cultural agencies unknown a few years before. The era came to a close in 1850 with a new one of railroads and iron ore carriers impending. Cleveland had grown greatly. New leaders had arisen. The mayor of the city in 1850, William Case, was the first native born son to attain a high position of leadership. The Arkites and others with some instinct for culture were in the high places.

CLEVELAND IN 1850 — In 1850 the people of Cincinnati could speak kindly of the young rival in the north. The editor of the *Cincinnati Gazette* had the following good words for Cleveland: "Cleveland is the most desirable town in the 'Great West' *to live in*. The town is clean, tasteful, elegant and healthful; for vegetables, fruit and flowers it is preeminent — for groves, parks, ornamental trees and shrubs, it is hardly surpassed by New Haven — and these attractions have drawn, and will continue to draw, hundreds and thousands thither — simply as the most comfortable and desirable place to live in. Her public and private schools are excellent; her medical college superior to any in the West, and the prevailing character of her society

7

educational, moral and religious. It is, therefore, 'just the spot' for the man of moderate income, to live and educate his family."[1]

THE GREEK REVIVAL IN ARCHITECTURE COMES TO CLEVELAND— The editor, who was reporting upon his observations from a recent visit saw two or three things which especially attracted him: (1) the general prosperity of the booming years of canal commerce, (2) the vast expansion of trees, which had already marked it as "The Forest City," and (3) the large number of homes of pleasing appearance. Nothing is a more distinctive feature of ante-bellum Cleveland than the multiplication of fine homes — evidence, of course, of the continuation of prosperous years through the decade of the 'fifties and into the Civil War, but also of good taste in architecture. At the end of the period, let us call it the period of the Greek Revival, and if we must fix a date, let it be between 1850 and 1870, a visitor standing in the middle of Superior Street, just east of Bond Street (East Sixth), looking westward, would have had a city view unmatched elsewhere, with few exceptions. There was a wide street leading to a forested public park. In the foreground on the left were the attractive homes of James Farmer, Frederick A. Sterling, Philo Chamberlain and Samuel A. Raymond, all business men of the day. In the background rose the spires of Trinity and the Second Presbyterian churches, and across the street, to the right, the Federal Post Office and Case Hall.

Or again, for another fine view, suppose the visitor took his position in the center of Euclid and Erie Streets. As he looked along the south side of Euclid Street westward, he would see the

1 One would think that Cleveland, too, must have appreciated its unique location, with a great lake at its front door. In fact the City Council had a short time before this given some evidence that it was planning to utilize its great asset. On September 1, 1847, the *Weekly Herald* made the statement that the City Council had moved to secure a "suitable spot immediately on the bank of the lake for a public park or promenade." In spite of some recent tendencies to build homes beyond the Public Square on Euclid, Prospect and Kinsman, North Water Street, St. Clair and Lake were still favorite resident streets with a magnificent view out over the lake. Iron mills and railroads had not taken over the lake front. The future beckoned, but in vain.

8

A View of Homes on Superior in the Greek Revival Period. Looking southwestward from a point in front of the present Hollenden Hotel. Residences of James Farmer, Fred A. Sterling, Philo Chamberlain, Henry A. Raymond. Sixth Street was cut through between the Chamberlain and Raymond homes. Trinity and Second Presbyterian Church in background.

The Greek Revival in Architecture has come to Cleveland. Home of T. P. Handy, built about 1842.
On site of Hippodrome Building.

Old Euclid Street of the 'Fifties and 'Sixties. From East Ninth (Erie), north side, westward. Homes of Lemuel Crawford, Martin B. Scott, Henry L. Gaylord, and Henry Chisholm.

A View of Euclid Street from about the site of the Old Higbee Building, eastward.
Euclid Street Presbyterian Church at Brownell (East 14). Homes of Samuel L. Mather
(later W. G. Mather), James F. Clark (later W. S. Tyler), and Henry H. Dodge
(now in back of the Bulkley Building.)

new City High School, the old Truman P. Handy residence, later occupied by the Union Club, and the Ursuline Convent, a girls' seminary, originally the home of Judge Samuel Cowles. Looking down the street on the north side, he would see the homes of Lemuel Crawford, Martin B. Scott, Henry L. Gaylord, and Henry Chisholm, all business men, with St. Paul's on the left in the distance, at Sheriff Street. Let us take our guest eastward on Euclid Street as far as Muirson (East 12th). Again looking westward along the north side of Euclid, there would come into view the residences of Stillman Witt, Lemuel Wick, O. M. Oviatt and S. B. Prentiss, railroad contractor, banker, capitalist and lawyer, respectively. Turning around eastward, looking along the north side of Euclid, the homes of Amasa Stone, W. J. Boardman, Zalmon Fitch, Selah Chamberlain, Sr., Samuel L. Mather, James F. Clark and Henry H. Dodge would be directly in the foreground, all fine examples of classical influences in Cleveland architecture; those of Boardman and Dodge with columns rising to the roof represented the Greek Revival in architecture at its best. In the distance on the south side at Brownell (East 14th), was the Euclid Street Presbyterian Church. Whichever way he looked on upper Superior or Euclid the prospect must have pleased. James F. Ryder, the Cleveland photographer, has described Euclid Street as he first saw it in the early 'fifties — "filled, not closely filled with residences, not a shop upon it. It was the road to Doan Corners, out Euclid way. I gave myself the pleasure many times of loitering past those beautiful houses."

Evidently men of skill and taste were planning and building the Cleveland of the decades of the 'fifties and 'sixties. A share of the credit should go to the architect-builders. As in the earlier years much of the better work was that of Jonathan A. Goldsmith or of his son-in-law, Charles W. Heard, or of Simeon C. Porter or Warham J. Warner. Goldsmith built the Judge Cowles residence, purchased later by the Ursuline Convent; he and Heard, the S. J. Andrews home; Warner, the Old Stone

Church as rebuilt in 1853. The prevailing style of architecture in Cleveland was Greek Revival, with imposing porticos across the front, after designs in the textbooks of eastern builders. Infinite variety appeared in the details — Doric, Ionic, or Corinthian columns. On the less fashionable streets, the simple, plain lines of the houses of the colonial period of the seaboard towns were everywhere visible. If good architecture in homes, churches and public buildings is an evidence of culture, then Cleveland at the middle of the nineteenth century represented a community of a relatively high degree of culture.

II. THE RAILROAD BRINGS A NEW ERA

SLOW EVOLUTION OF A PRACTICAL RAILROAD — TRACKS, CARS, ENGINES — The rapid development of the railroad in the decade from 1850-1860 introduced a new era in American economic history. It had required a quarter of a century to develop the early experiments with locomotives, coaches and strip rails into a practical means of transportation. The approaches to many cities were strewn with the wrecks of visionary projects, like the piles that marked the approaches to Cleveland on the site of the defunct Ohio Railroad. Naturally private capital was slow to venture into such speculative projects. Most of the early railroads secured assistance from the towns or states which they served. Nearly half of the capital stock of the Baltimore and Ohio Railroad came from subscriptions by Maryland and Virginia, Baltimore and Wheeling, the remainder from the business men of Baltimore City.

EASTERN RAILROAD BUILDERS REACH THE INLAND WATERWAYS— New York City and Philadelphia had waterways reaching the interior of the continent, partly natural water courses, partly state built canals. For a time Cleveland with the Ohio and the P. & O. canals could, like New York City and Philadelphia, be quite complacent. But Baltimore, Charleston and Boston could not be satisfied with their situations. Their business men built the first sections of the Baltimore & Ohio, the Charleston & Hampden, the Boston & Worcester and the Boston & Providence railroads, doing for their trade a small part of what the Erie Canal and the Pennsylvania chain of waterways were doing for New York City and Philadelphia. In the 'thirties and 'forties the Charleston road reached Hampden on the Savannah River, the Boston roads, not only Worcester and Providence, but Albany and New York City, and the Baltimore line nearly to the crest of the Alleghenies, at Cumberland. The growing evidence that the railroad had advantages canals could not offer shook the canal cities out of their complacency. A general awakening occurred about 1845 or 1846. The building of railroads became an order of the day. In five or six years the transportation map of America took on a new appearance, at least that of the northern states.

In 1851 the New York and Erie Railroad, later known as the Erie, was completed to Dunkirk on Lake Erie, the first to bind the Atlantic coast with the interior of the continent. The following year, the Pennsylvania Railroad, paralleling the Pennsylvania system of waterways, reached Pittsburgh. A year later, the Baltimore and Ohio, after a heroic struggle of 33 years, was finished to the Ohio River at Wheeling. In the same year the several interurban lines between Albany and Buffalo were combined into the New York Central Railroad. As a result the East was joined with the West in four great lines. The urban requirements for an all year service had brought about a general transition from canals to railroads.

In Ohio, aside from one or two local lines, the first important railroad, that from Sandusky to Cincinnati through Tiffin and Springfield, had been completed in 1848. It had been with some justice that Ohio had subsidized the Mad River Railroad, as the line was popularly called, subscribing $270,000 to its capital. The Ohio system of canals, built and maintained by the state, had left that section of Ohio unserved by transportation facilities. But by 1845 the state was overburdened with canal and turnpike debts, nearing bankruptcy in fact. As a result, in 1851, the dele-

gates in the Ohio constitutional convention imposed severe re-
strictions on state aid to private corporations or on state under-
takings in the line of public works on its own account. Cleveland
and other cities of Ohio were obliged to work out other means of
attracting capital into railroad building. They did so generally
by taking stock in whatever project came along, some deserving,
many not.

CLEVELAND'S NEW ARTERIES OF BUSINESS LIFE — Cleveland voted
to subscribe to the stock of each of the companies organized
to join it with its neighbors: $200,000 to the Cleveland, Columbus
and Cincinnati; $100,000 each to the Cleveland and Pittsburgh
through Hudson and Alliance, and to the Cleveland and Erie
through Painesville and Ashtabula. All were completed at
approximately the same time the eastern railroads reached
Lake Erie and the Ohio River, between 1851 and 1853. On
March 29, 1853, the *Cleveland Daily True Democrat* announced
a "lightning train" between Cleveland and Cincinnati in eight
hours, and a few weeks later a similar train to Buffalo in six and
one half hours. The T rails of iron came from England, the
locomotives were built in the works of the Cuyahoga Steam
Furnace Company in Ohio City. In many cases the leading con-
tractors for the Cleveland railroads, Frederick Harbach, Amasa
Stone and Stillman Witt, were obliged to take the principal
portion of their pay in the stock of the railroad companies.

Within a few years two other lines filled out important links
in the national pattern of transportation—The Cleveland and
Toledo, a link in the service from New York to Chicago, and the
Cleveland and Mahoning, after 1863 a part of the Erie system, giving Cleveland access to the coal fields around Youngstown.

It required the expanding telegraph lines to make railroad
operation completely safe and efficient. In that process Jeptha
H. Wade and others had taken up the invention of Samuel F. B.
Morse and given it practical uses by means of many telegraph
lines. About 1856, having become general agent for the newly

organized Western Union Telegraph Company, Wade took up his residence in Cleveland, adding another to the rising group of business and cultural leaders. The railroads coming into Cleveland were the immediate gainers.

In Cleveland there was some heart burning over the entrance of railroads into the city. Some wanted the terminus of the Cleveland, Columbus and Cincinnati in Cleveland Center in the valley, on Columbus Road, at the edge of town. Until after the Civil War the Cleveland and Toledo Railroad was held to a small station on the west side of the Cuyahoga, ferrying its passengers over the river. The editor of the *Plain Dealer* said he liked the "outside location of the depots." Nor was the idea of a station on the lake shore liked any better. Wouldn't commerce pass *through* the city rather than stop in it for the benefit of Cleveland merchants? In the Old Stone Church there were those who sought to restrain their fellows from subscribing to the stock of the railroads. Wouldn't they run their trains on Sunday? The City Council passed an ordinance to limit the speed of trains within the city limits to four miles an hour, in order that a team of horses might find time to walk out of the way.

THE ANNUAL WINTER HIBERNATION COMES TO AN END—The rejoicing, however, over the changes effected by the railroads was well nigh universal. Only canal operators, stage coach owners and tavern keepers had cause to be unhappy over the intrusion of the railroads. Stage coach lines were the first casualties of the railroad era, being put out of business almost overnight and forced to sell their equipment or allow it to mold and ultimately pass into museums for the history of transportation. The coming of the railroads marked for all practical purposes the beginning of the rapid passing of the Ohio canal system. It might drag on for a generation, a dying system, but dying it was. Canal Days in Cleveland were over. The Railroad Era had come, and it was high time. Dr. John S. Newberry described the meaning of the new railroads to Cleveland. "The effect has been magical, the increase in business with each month, twelve months in the year. We no longer have an annual hibernation. It is no longer necessary that the existance of a Clevelander should be extended thirty-three percent beyond the common term, in order that he should have his share of life." In the unification of the north, east and west of the Alleghenies, the revolution was to have a profound meaning in the approaching crisis of the Civil War.

III. THE IRON ORE CARRIERS COME TO CLEVELAND

CLEVELAND IRON ORE COMPANIES — Other events of the early 'fifties were giving shape to things which were important for Cleveland; events which would soon determine the social as well as the economic or industrial life of all Clevelanders. The story of how Cleveland business men came to found the iron ore trade is fascinating. The pioneer phases came in the Canal Days. The Cleveland Iron Mining Company, chartered in 1853, was the first in the field. Its development under the leadership of Samuel L. Mather and his son, William G. Mather, into the Cleveland Cliffs Iron Company and the separate organization of Pickands-Mather — Samuel Mather, another son, and James Pickands — to enter fields of iron ore other than the Marquette Range, are all a part of the history of Cleveland.

In 1851 Henry B. Tuttle began business in Cleveland as a commission merchant, interested in the prospects for the iron ore trade. For several years he was secretary of the Cleveland Iron Mining Company, but he withdrew to go into the iron mining and shipping business on his own account. How his son, after his death, drew into their organization Earl W. Oglebay and how later David Z. Norton joined them are stages in the evolution of Oglebay, Norton and Company. This is a story of 1890, how Norton and Oglebay came together.[2] In the Marquette Range the Jackson Iron Company was, from the first, a rival of the

2 See the *Cleveland Plain Dealer*, May 24, 1937.

Cleveland Iron Mining Company. In 1862 Fayette Brown, a banker, destined to be another of the leaders in making the city on the Cuyahoga an iron center, became the general manager of the Jackson Iron Company. Many years later the Jackson organization's mines were purchased by the Cleveland Cliffs Iron Company.

For Cleveland business history and the rise of the iron and coal trade it was also significant that Hanna, Garretson and Company, which meant Leonard and Robert Hanna and Hiram Garretson, had left New Lisbon, Ohio, and were now in Cleveland, already in the mid-'fifties engaged in coal mining and shipping and in operating boats to the Lake Superior trading posts. Apparently from the record sometime in the summer of 1850 Leonard Hanna and Mrs. Hanna visited the new mining towns of Lake Superior. It would seem that the voyage turned the interests of the Hanna family more definitely toward the rising Lake Superior iron and coal trade. In any event, the resources of the Hannas came to be united with those of Daniel P. Rhodes, through the marriage of Marcus A. Hanna to Augusta Rhodes, in the coal and iron business of northern Ohio and the Great Lakes. In time Rhodes & Co., became the M. A. Hanna Company. As finally organized it was in a strategic position to enter the field along with the other concerns and together make Cleveland a great industrial city, based on the meeting of iron and coal.

THE EVOLUTION OF THE IRON ORE CARRIERS — The early shipments of iron ore from the Marquette mines were in small sailing ships, barques or brigantines, tramp ships, chartered for the season. The Historical Society has the bill of lading for the first shipment of iron ore to Cleveland, six barrels in 1852.[3] The Cleveland Iron Mining Company's first ship was a brigantine (*Columbia*) of 550 tons capacity. In 1855 it carried the first load of ore through the Soo Canal. In 1872 a line of wooden freight steamers with a capacity of 1,000 tons each was acquired.

3 Shipment by the Marquette Iron Company, an organization acquired afterwards by the Cleveland Iron Mining Company. W. H. R. S., Mss. 2825.

Sixteen years later the company built its first steel steamboats, especially designed for the iron ore trade, and the development of the remarkable iron ore carriers had started.

THE SOO CANAL AND THE GREAT LAKES — A MAJOR BUSINESS ARTERY — In 1855 Michigan, aided by a land grant from the United States, opened for use the St. Mary's ship canal, thus connecting Lake Superior and Lake Huron for shipping purposes. It was a public work, indispensable if iron was to be economically shipped from the ore fields of the upper peninsula to the furnaces of Ohio and Pennsylvania. By 1858 Captain Alva Bradley was operating a fleet of brigs and schooners to carry ore direct from the Michigan ports to Cleveland. The completion of the Iron Mountain Railroad from Marquette to the mines shortly afterwards was an event of little less importance. The problem of unloading ore in port, was solved later. Instead of unloading by wheel barrows and gangplank with great toil and delay, Alexander E. Brown, son of Fayette Brown, developed about 1880 the system of hoisting and conveying by machinery. He built for this purpose in Cleveland the Old Tom Collins, followed in turn by the Brown hoist system and thus introduced a remarkable phase in the development of the iron ore business. Others perfected a system of loading the carriers by gravity. But these events are a later story in the romance of iron ore shipping. Before the Civil War iron ore from Lake Superior had begun to have a part in the industrial life of Cleveland. Indeed, the decade of the 'fifties saw many changes in Cleveland.

IV. THE UNION OF OHIO CITY AND CLEVELAND

TWO IN ONE—In 1854 Cleveland and Ohio City united. Such a union, logical as it was, had been long delayed by petty differences between the two cities. The Battle of the Bridges, over whether there should be but one bridge and that on Columbus Street, or two, another on Center Street, had caused much ill feeling on both sides. In 1851 a popular vote on union failed to

The Classical Influence on Cleveland Architecture at its best. The George Worthington residence, built about 1852. On the site of the Arena.

From the Greek Revival to the Victorian Period. On left, Stillman Witt residence, built about 1852. On right, home of Witt's son-in-law, Colonel Wm. Harris, built about 1880. Latter on site of Hotel Statler.

carry, but three years later public opinion decidedly approved the plan of both city councils for union. Mayor William B. Castle of Ohio City became the first mayor of the united cities, evidence of a new time of good feelings, the majority generously allowing the minority the honors at the start.

THE CHARTER MAKERS TAKE DEMOCRACY SERIOUSLY — The charter makers had adopted the ideals of the Jacksonian democracy, allowing the voters to take unto themselves the choice of all their local officials. As a result at election time any city of Ohio was a perfect jungle, perfect for the politicians, a bewildering maze for the voters. In 1855 Clevelanders elected a mayor, two trustees or councilmen for each ward, a city marshall, a civil engineer, a city commissioner, a fire engineer, city treasurer, assessor, auditor, solicitor, prosecuting attorney, police judge, street commissioner, director of the infirmary, commissioner of water works, superintendent of markets, harbor master, city sealer, weigher of hay, and a sexton. Perhaps it was with some justice that the *Cleveland Leader* (February 3, 1855) called Cleveland the worst governed city in the union. Why it was worse than other cities of Ohio of the same class is not apparent in the record.

SOME CITY IMPROVEMENTS — WATER WORKS AND BRIDGES — As a part of the bargain of the union, the greater Cleveland built the Main Street bridge, another one at the foot of Seneca Street hill and rebuilt the Center Street bridge. It also went on to widen and deepen the "Old River Bed," significant improvements in cementing the ties between the east and the west of Cleveland. Just before the union of the two cities, Cleveland (in 1853) had decided to build a water system. The committee on a water supply was the mayor, William Case, Warham J. Warner of the firm of Heard and Warner, architects and builders, Jared P. Kirtland and Colonel Charles Whittlesey, scientist and civil engineer, respectively. They chose Lake Erie as a better source of supply of pure water than Mill Creek, Shaker Run, Tinker's Creek, or the Cuyahoga River. Three years later water flowed in the city's mains and the favorite drinking well on the northwest corner of the Public Square like the other town wells, passed into history.

The water works, railroads and plank roads were only a local part of a new era in American history. Industrial expansion and changes in the manufacturing processes in Cleveland were the local phase of a national movement which had set in after the Mexican War. In fact, the Mexican War had only delayed the process. Now that the nation had recovered from the long depression that followed 1837, forces were set for a continuation of the expansion of the early 'thirties. Raw materials, capital, labor, management and a better system of transportation were a great combination. The barriers of money differences had been removed. In Ohio a new banking system would have a part. For Cleveland and Pittsburgh, and many other cities, the availability of iron ore and coal were to determine the local character of the industrial expansion.

V. CLEVELAND BECOMES A MANUFACTURING CENTER

THE EARLY IRON MILLS — In the field of iron manufacturers alone the expansion had been very large. The first City Directory, that of 1837, gave Cleveland and Ohio City together six iron foundries, boiler works, and steam engine manufacturers. In 1860 there were more than a score of such works, larger than ever, and several of them the foundations of corporations in existence eighty years later. To those of 1837 had been added mills which would make Cleveland quite an industrial center. Of the older institutions the Cuyahoga Steam Furnace Company, founded in 1834, manufacturing locomotives, boilers and other iron products, was well established, William B. Castle, President. Both George Worthington and W. A. Otis, dealers in hardware entered into the manufacturing of their own products — Otis in 1840 to make iron castings, Worthington in 1846 to make bar iron. Otis' son, Charles A. Otis, in partnership with J. N. Ford, erected a steam forge, making a variety of forgings, axles for railroad cars and locomotives and heavy shafts for steamboats. In the early 'fifties they added a rolling mill to manufacture boiler plate, using for the purpose Lake Erie iron ore. This plant, the Lake Erie Iron Works, was located on the old river bed, near the lake shore. In 1859 it became Otis & Company. In the meantime Otis had added a rolling mill to manufacture merchant bar, etc.

Out in Newburgh and in Cleveland, Henry Chisholm, like Andrew Carnegie a Scotchman and iron master, had bar and railroad rolling mills, which would later become a part of a great industry. (Really at this time it was Stone, Chisholm and Jones Company). Samuel L. Mather of the Cleveland Iron Mining Company, prepared to supply iron ore, was president of the Cleveland Plate Boiler Company, thus entering the field of iron manufacture. On the lake shore, near Case Avenue, was the Railroad Iron Mill Company, later a part of the Cleveland Rolling Mill. The Cleveland Directory of 1858 lists several of the manufacturers of iron products in one form or another, two paper mills, copper smelting and white lead works, melodeon and furniture factories and stove works, altogether enough to give evidence that an industrial era had begun in Cleveland. Six hundred and fifty men were employed in the iron industry. The Cleveland Rolling Mill employed 125 men and manufactured 147 T rails a day.

After the completion of the Soo Canal an abundance of iron ore from upper Michigan became available and, of course, stimulated the development of the iron industry in Cleveland in all its forms, from the furnaces and foundries through rolling mills and a great variety of special processes. The opening of the Briarhill coal mines near Youngstown by David Tod and Daniel P. Rhodes was an important factor in the development of industries in Cleveland. Before 1857 the coal was brought to Cleveland by the P. and O. Canal, afterwards on the Cleveland and Mahoning Railroad. The editors of the newspapers complained of the backwardness of Cleveland business men in starting blast furnaces which would ease the dependence of manufacturers on outside sources — Youngstown and Pittsburgh, for example. None-the-less, there had been a general awakening in Cleveland as to the possibilities in iron manufacturing.

WHERE BANKS HAVE A SHARE — Naturally the expansion in business had been accompanied by a need for larger banking facilities. Or, to put it from the point of view of a banker, the increase in bank deposits had been one of the factors in business expansion. Both were true: larger business, larger banks; larger banks, larger business became possible. The Minutes of the City Bank show the leaders in many of the new enterprises among its customers for loans. The City Bank had not long been alone in the field. It had opened its doors for business just at the beginning of the new era in Cleveland history, July 1, 1845. Eight days later the Bank of Ohio opened a Cleveland branch — the Merchant's Bank, in the Atwater Building. The following year, as though one branch of the state system was not enough, a second branch was opened, January, 1846 — the Commercial Branch Bank. It was also located in the Atwater Building, beside its associate — William A. Otis, president, T. P. Handy, cashier. A few months later the Merchant's Bank moved to the Weddell House, in a new home with a new president, Sherlock J. Andrews, who had succeeded P. M. Weddell. An independent bank, the Canal Bank, opened its doors for business during the same year, 1846, in the Merchant's Exchange Building at the foot of Superior, organized especially to serve the needs of canal shippers. Whatever may have been the real cause of failure, the Canal Bank went down a few years later, with the shifting of shipping from the canals to the railroads.[4]

A bank, unique in organization and purpose, was organized in 1849 — the Society for Savings. It was in effect a mutual society for savings, particularly small savings. It was opened in a small room on Bank Street, with a tin box for a vault. It was

[4] Several paragraphs like this one have been reprinted from my History of the National City Bank — A Century of Progress — by the courtesy of the National City Bank of Cleveland.

unique in having no capital stock and in its system of distributing its profits among its depositors. The first president was John W. Allen, its secretary Samuel H. Mather. Two independent banks were organized in 1853 — The Forest City Bank (which failed during the Civil War) and the Bank of Commerce, not to be confused with the Branch Bank of Commerce. President Joseph Perkins was long associated with the Bank of Commerce.

The climax in this period of expansion of banking facilities was the organization in 1858 of Cleveland's first Clearing House Association. Its purpose was "to affect at one place, and in the most economical and safe manner, the daily exchange between the several associated banks and bankers (private bankers as distinguished from incorporated banks) the maintenance of uniform rates for eastern exchange, and the regulation of what descriptions of funds shall be paid and received in the settlement of business." Of this institution the City Bank was a member, and one of its founders. T. P. Handy, at the moment cashier of the Commercial Branch Bank, was the first president of the association. Handy, Lemuel Wick, president of the City Bank, and Fayette Brown, a private banker, constituted the executive committee.

INTERRUPTED BY A PANIC — The City Directory of 1858 lists two state branch banks, four independent banks and fourteen private bankers. Bank Street was called the Wall Street of Cleveland because of the number of banking houses which had been located thereon at one time or another. The record of the establishment of new banks and their growing assets tells the story of Cleveland's growth as effectively as does that of the statistics of the iron and coal industry. But in Cleveland as elsewhere in the United States, and abroad as well, expansion of railways, industries and business houses generally had been too rapid to continue without a break. The failure in 1857 of a large Cincinnati banking house caused a temporary panic, and this and other failures throughout the nation affected banks, merchants, manufacturers and business men with large payments to make. The whole population suffered with them, of course. In New York City sixteen banks failed.

Apparently Clevelanders had learned their lesson in the previous panic and remembered it. For a while specie was scarce and banks stopped making loans, except for short term and on the best of security. At one time a run on the Commercial Bank started a near bank panic, but President Joseph Perkins publicly requested the depositors to withdraw all their deposits. As might be expected the challenge turned the tide; the depositors asked that they be allowed to leave their money where it was. The Cleveland banks weathered the storm safely, and so far as the record shows, business houses generally. A week after the panic the *Cleveland Leader* could say "the feeling is now quite calm, comparatively, in this city, and things are rapidly resuming their accustomed channels." On October 12, the same newspaper expressed the view that the City Bank was "abundantly able to meet the most pressing demand." There was no run upon it. Of the Panic of 1857 the Cleveland Board of Trade wrote: "We believe not one manufactory closed its doors for want of work; a few were run to their full capacity." But the following sentence recorded where the panic hurt: "For most of them the number of employees was reduced from 25 to 50 percent."

FROM THE OMNIBUS TO THE STREET RAILWAY — As the decade closed the omnibus gave way to horse drawn street cars. Justus Cozad recollected that Ed Duty began to run an omnibus twice daily between the City Hotel and the Croton House in 1853, fare ten cents, and that he afterwards extended his trip to Euclid Creek. This was the beginning of regular passenger service on Euclid Street, unless one had been able to find a place on the four horse stages between Cleveland and eastern points. The *Cleveland Herald* of 1860 gave the schedules of the city omnibus lines. From Cleveland to Collamer, via St. Clair Street, an omnibus left the City Hall at 4:30 P.M., Collamer at 7:30 A.M., fare 20 cents; from Cleveland to the Croton House, East Cleveland, two trips daily along Euclid Street, leaving the Commercial Hotel at 11 A.M. and 4 P.M.; similar lines ran twice a day on Kinsman (Woodland) as far as the Cleveland Female Seminary near Case Street, and on the West Side to the Reservoir on Franklin Street.

In 1859, after overcoming much opposition in the City Council, two companies received authority to build street railways, one the East Cleveland line and the other Kinsman. The East Cleveland line, planned to extend to Doan Corners, was completed in 1860 to the city limits at Willson and Euclid; the other out Kinsman as far as Willson (East 55th). Both were horse car lines, using both single and double horse-cars. The iron was supplied by the Newburgh mills. Three years later a West side line connected Pearl and Lorain Streets with the Square. By 1860 the editor of the *Cleveland Leader* could say that it was no longer necessary for citizens "to plod the way through our almost bottomless streets nearly half the year."

Ten years brought many changes. The coming of the railroads, of new natural resources like iron and coal, the development of manufactories, and especially the iron furnaces, forges and rolling mills, foreshadowed great industrial changes. Even oil and gas, soon to be added to the city's natural resources, were crowding onto the attention of the readers of newspapers. The *Cleveland Leader* early in 1861 reported the discovery of oil and gas in many parts of the Western Reserve, and particularly the excitement over oil in Trumbull County and the fever symptoms known best to the Forty-niners of California. But few in Cleveland yet saw the significance for the community of springs of black oil and seeping gas. They could be seen any day on Kinsman Street. Such things had been seen in many places since the day Moses Cleaveland touched a light to the bubbling waters at the mouth of Euclid Creek. It troubled the editors that the city council and the ever-pressing letter writers indicted the rolling mills because they smoked, and would prohibit coal oil refineries because they smelt bad.

VI. CULTURAL DEVELOPMENTS DURING THE 'FIFTIES

NEW ELEMENTS OF POPULATION ENTER THE CITY — From every point of view the 'fifties constituted the early stages, for Cleveland, of an industrial revolution. The population had grown from 21,000 in 1850, including Ohio City, to 43,800 in 1860 — an increase of 113 percent. The federal census of 1850 was the first one to give the place of birth of the population. According to that 45 percent of the population of Cleveland was of German, Irish or British birth. In Ohio City more than half of the population had recently come from abroad. The coming of the new elements fed the needs of the mills and factories as they were established, and accounts in a large measure for the prosperity of the period. The history of Cleveland was to be deeply affected by the nativity of its inhabitants, advancing in some ways and retarding in others the intellectual development. In education the newcomers into the American sphere had seldom had the advantages of the natives. In the fine arts — music, the graphic arts and the theatre — they had acquired in their homelands not only an interest but in some cases high degrees of skill.

THE RELIGIOUS ASPECT — Whatever the significance of the addition of new elements of population, and we shall see they were marked, the religious aspects were profoundly changed. A large proportion, probably a large majority, were from Catholic Europe and continued to be loyal to their earlier faith. Bishop Rappe of the Northern Ohio Diocese was confronted with the almost superhuman task of meeting the needs of his parishioners. In the 'forties there had been one Catholic Church for Cuyahoga County — St. Mary's on the "flats", on Columbus Street, in "Cleveland Center." St. John's Cathedral at Superior and Erie was completed in 1852. Two years later, to accommodate the oncoming tide of Germans, St. Mary's was allotted to their use, and a new church on Superior beyond the cathedral, St. Peter's, as well. For the Irish, St. Patrick's on the West Side beyond Franklin Circle was dedicated at about the same time. In rapid succession others followed in neighborhoods occupied predominantly by Irish, German and English speaking Catholics. Cleveland could no longer regard itself as peculiarly a New England community, or Puritanic in religious outlook.

In the larger Cleveland of 1860 there were nine Methodist churches, four Catholic, four Episcopal, six Presbyterian, three Baptist, three Lutheran, two Congregational, two Jewish and one Disciples. New church buildings had replaced the first structures of the pioneer days, some of them notable for architectural grace and richness of the interiors; but poor imitations of old world models of previous centuries. Old Stone of 1853, rebuilt in 1858 after a fire, and Trinity of 1855 were substantial stone structures; the spires more sightly, reached farther heavenward than their predecessors. Most of the new churches were shifting their sites with the changing trends of city expansion. Trinity moved over from St. Clair to Superior, nearly opposite the end of the Bond Street of that day. The Second Presbyterian (1852) was built a few doors westward, nearer the Square, and in sight of Old Stone Church — not to be facetious, a stone's throw. St. Paul's a second Episcopal church, was built on Euclid at Sheriff, again a short distance from the parent association, Trinity Church. Explain, if you can, this tendency of offshoots of older congregations to settle barely a block away. The First Baptist Church moved from Seneca and Champlain to Euclid and Erie, northwest corner. A decade later the First Methodist followed the trend by moving from St. Clair and Wood (East Third) to Euclid and Erie, the southeast corner.

The Cleveland directories of the 'fifties carried information about the organization and work of the Young Men's Christian Association, organized in 1854, and the Ladies' Christian Union, 1859. Dr. John S. Newberry was the first president of the Y. M.-

C. A. Among the others who had a part in its organization were Solon L. Severance, Loren Prentiss, Joseph B. Merriam, Daniel P. Eels, James M. Hoyt, and Samuel H. Mather. The Association maintained a yearly lecture course. Both organizations sought to give to youth moral and cultural influences the churches could not furnish. With immigration and material progress the church congregations had grown, but not as might have been expected.

The strangers had introduced amusing differences of speech, destined slowly to be the basis for a new language, not quite British, America's own tongue. On Christmas day, 1851, Cleveland Protestants were surprised to learn that Pastor Henry Schwan of Zion Church, the German Lutheran Church on York Street (now the center of the site of the Public Hall) had introduced in his Christmas service an unheard of innovation — nothing less than an evergreen tree decorated with candles, gilt, tinsel, candies and apples. To the great body of New Englanders, Congregational and Presbyterian, it was a "heathenish custom", a "pagan absurdity," a plain case of idolatry, "groveling before shrubs." Some were for seeing that it didn't happen again, but in the end reason prevailed and Pastor Schwan's custom became a part of a happier American life.[5]

THE NEWCOMER — The arrival in the late 'forties and 'fifties of new elements from the British Isles and Europe, unencumbered with some of the inhibitions of the Puritans, gave a marked impulse to the development of interest in all the fine arts, and music in particular. If one wanted material evidence, the several new assembly halls of the period would serve. Brainard's Hall on Superior, over his music store, 77 Superior, formerly Watson's Hall (named for the builder), later became the Melodeon, then again the Athenaeum and later the Globe Theater. As the Athenaeum it was a popular hall in the 'fifties. But names of public halls had a way of changing with the moon,

5 Hertha Pauli, The Story of the Christmas Tree, Boston, 1944. The Reverend Henry C. Schwan has left an account. See *Cleveland Leader*, Nov. 16, 1902. It seems that since 1848 lighted Christmas trees had been seen in German homes in Wooster, O.

doubtless a sign of a tenuous existence. The Academy of Music
(1852) on Bank Street, between St. Clair and Superior, intended
as a theater, called variously the National Hall, Cleveland Theater,
and Foster's Theater, after the name of a lessee, came to have
more than a local reputation as a center of musical and theatrical
affairs. "Quite a dream of beauty it was and a pride to Clevelanders," so said Ryder, the photographer. It was here that Uncle
John Ellsler began his Cleveland career. The Academy of Music
had the distinction of being heated with a furnace. Chapin's Hall,
known as the Concert Hall, was also built in the early 'fifties
and was considered by local writers one of the finest halls in the
United States. It would seat 1,200 persons. Located at the
southeast corner of the Public Square, it, in common with other
halls and churches, showed the tendency of the time to move
places of public assembly away from Water Street and St. Clair
with the eastward movement of residences.

In 1854 the organization of the Gesengverein by the Germans,
superseding the Frohsinn of the 'forties, was an important event
in the musical history of Cleveland. Under its auspices Saengerfests, national German musical festivals, three day affairs, were
held in 1854 and again in 1859. In the first case 300 singers, and
in the second 400, contested for prizes. Such musical events
attracted national interest, so the Cleveland newspapers reported,
and other evidence supports their eulogies.

The second Saengerfest closed with the grand opera "Alesandro
Stradella" in the Academy of Music. Later in the year the Parodi
Italian opera troupe was at the Academy of Music in grand
opera. *The Cleveland Leader*, November 2, 1859, thought it a great
success "in excellent tone and spirit." On the last night the
opera was well attended, so the editor says, but he adds, "the
admission price was cut from one dollar to fifty cents."

Less exotic was the organization of the Cleveland Mendelssohn
Society (1851) formed to elevate the standard of sacred music.
Truman P. Handy was president, J. L. Severance vice president,
J. F. Hanks, professor of music. There was not one German in

its organization. New Connecticut was aroused for its own honor and in its own way. The Society claimed to have one hundred vocal performers and an orchestra of twenty-five pieces. Hanks received his professional title from the newspapers because he operated a singing academy. Other teachers of music had similar aspirations. In 1854 and again in 1856 R. B. Wheeler and E. A. Payne announced musical instruction in the Cleveland Academy of Music. The school soon disappeared, leaving no trace of its activities or influence.

In October 1858 the *Cleveland Plain Dealer* promoted a project to purchase the old Round Church of the Millerites on St. Clair for a music school. Nothing came of that and musical instruction remained an activity of individual teachers. Concerts by their pupils, by teachers' musical conventions, church concerts and by the several musical societies — St. Cecilia, Germanis, Cleveland Musical Society, Cuyahoga County Musical Society, the Euphonians, the Cleveland Choral Union, the Cleveland Philharmonic Society, the Cleveland Musical Union, a west side institution — were regular features of a season that now lasted throughout the year. But the occasions each year that made musical history before the Civil War were the appearance of such stars as Jenny Lind, Catherine Hayes, Ole Bull and Adelina Patti. From small beginnings in the Canal Days the developments of the new railroad era looked auspicious indeed.

ART — Writing in 1910 on the history of art in Cleveland, Carl Lorenz said, "Half a century ago there was no art life in Cleveland. Here and there a young man or woman might have been found struggling with brush and palette, full of enthusiasm and perhaps not without talent. The atmosphere was missing and in many cases also the schooling. Even architecture was a thing of the future at that time and the fine arts were represented by a very few real paintings in the homes of a very few lovers of art to be found in Cleveland. One or two wood carvers and three or four clever stone cutters, foreigners by birth, constituted the art colony of our city, reminiscent of log cabins and wooden shanties."

Apparently in 1910 the period of the classical revival in architecture in Cleveland (1850-1870) was as unknown as the buried cities of ancient times, having given way to the Victorian. What he said about the work of the wood carvers and stone cutters was fairly accurate. In the 'fifties and 'sixties the Herkomers, fresh from Bavaria, were adorning the interiors of the homes of Amasa Stone, Frederick A. Sterling, Sherlock J. Andrews and numerous others with fine wood carvings. William Walcott had designed the statue of Commodore Perry and a stone cutter had executed it (1859). Ante-bellum Cleveland was far from the village of pioneer days or even the canal days. Nor was the art colony quite insignificant. The Cleveland Directory of 1857 includes six professional artists, several of them like Allen Smith, Jr. and Julius Gollman with notable achievements. J. F. Hanks must have been a real artist, for he made regular southern tours in the winter season. A number of them as teachers announced schools of art. For several years Josiah Humphrey was teacher of drawing and painting at the Cleveland Female Seminary and maintained at home an academy of drawing and painting, hours from 2:00 to 6:00 P.M. According to the newspapers others attempted to develop from individual to class instructors, always the first phase of mass education. There was Miss Noble's school of drawing and painting in her studio in Hoffman's Block and Alfred Boisseau's portrait and landscape classes. A teacher's studio was usually the May Show of the day.

Sometimes an art dealer suddenly became the possessor of an art gallery, either because a local artist deposited his wares in his store or because reproductions of the work of some foreign artist had become available. A regular feature in the newspapers was the announcement of travelling exhibitions of paintings, engravings or other art objects. The *Cleveland Daily True Democrat*, July 7, 1853, announced Rossiter's exhibition of historical paintings at the Academy of Music, admission twenty-five cents.

The exhibition included "The Return of the Dove" and "The Captive Isrealites." At another time Dubufe's "Adam and Eve," painted for Charles X, representing the "greatest event in human history," was on exhibition at Kelley's Hall on Superior Street, a hall that also tried to attain the hopeful name of Cleveland's Athenaeum.

Of more significance for the history of art were the public lectures of George Willey on the fine arts. Culture was taking a hold on the intellectual group of the day. Just at the close of the decade (1859) Julius Gollman, a German artist, painted the "Arkites" for William Case. It represented the Arkites in characteristic pose in one of their informal meetings in the Ark. The artist was paid four hundred dollars for his work. In his column in the *Plain Dealer* Artemus Ward called it an inimitable picture of "ye gallant Arkites." It was later presented to the Historical Society by Levi T. Scofield and hangs over the mantel in the Society's large reference room. The Society also possesses the pencil drawings and water color sketches, prepared by the artist preliminary to the group painting. In the history of cultural progress it is an invaluable record.

THE THEATER — The announcements in the daily newspapers leave no doubt about the larger part the theater had come to play in the 'fifties. Prosperous years and increased population tempted theatrical managers. The Academy of Music and the Athenaeum, more comfortable and attractive halls, were factors in better audiences and better plays. A brief but rather bizarre event occurred in 1853. P. T. Barnum came to Cleveland — not in person, but through representatives. His showmanship was for a few months a part of the Cleveland theatrical history. His agents purchased Irad Kelley's Hall, opposite the end of Bank Street, next to the American House, and his dramatic company appeared for a season. The newspapers recorded crowded halls and high praise, but, like so many of Barnum's enterprises of the period outside of New York City, it was short lived. John

Ellsler tells how near Barnum came to forcing his company into bankruptcy.

A more significant event was the coming to Cleveland of John Ellsler. A Philadelphian by birth, after several years on the stage, including some time with Joseph Jefferson, Ellsler sought to settle down in Cleveland as a resident actor-manager. In the spring of 1855 he leased the Academy of Music and, with his wife, Effie Ellsler, and a stock company of associates, offered the community a test of its interest in the theater. For three years he and Effie worked hard and continuously with scarcely a seasonal break. Measured by the succession of plays the newspapers carried, it was an astonishing record. On January 16, 1856, *The Cleveland Leader* said of Mrs. Ellsler's work on one occasion, "She played charmingly 'Cleveland in 1956,' presenting the ideals of the ladies in 1856, sporting silk hats, patent leathers and the rest." It was a common practice to combine a serious or long play with a short comedy or a farce. "Hamlet" might be coupled with "Family Jars" or a fantasy such as "Cleveland in 1960," or again, "Henry VIII" and the popular comedy "Still Waters Run Deep." It is clear from the record that the Academy of Music dominated the situation.

The Ellslers gave Cleveland a notable variety of plays — Shakesperian and popular types of the seaboard theaters. They gave their audiences an opportunity to see on the stage famous actors of the day like Edwin Forrest, Charlotte Cushman, James W. Wallack, Jr., and Miss Davenport, and also local players — opportunities otherwise unattainable.

In 1858 the Ellslers abandoned management and took to the road. The following year they returned twice to the Academy with a travelling company presenting "The Rivals" and "The Road to Bath" and "Our American Cousin," the Ellslers sustaining the principal characters. As the house was only fair it could not have greatly encouraged them. The following year Ellsler leased a theater in Cincinnati where he was at the opening of the Civil War. Much of the time after he left Cleveland the Academy of

Music was closed. For one thing Ellsler had had to face heavy license taxes. For several months in 1856 he was forced to close the theater on account of a prohibitive tax. Probably the hard times of 1857 was a factor; perhaps the prices of admission too high. Charges at the Academy of Music varied from one dollar to fifty cents for a seat in the dress circle and parquet, fifty cents to thirty-five cents for the family circle and twenty-five cents for the gallery. For small boxes the rate was five dollars, for large ten dollars. Ellsler's successor tried lower rates but with no better results. Perhaps Artemus Ward knew the real cause of Ellsler's financial failure. According to his view the older Clevelanders still thought the theater a "sink of ungodliness", and the newcomers who might have thought differently were too poor to be its patrons. In 1858 Horace Greeley said from the platform of the Melodeon that he considered Shakespeare a man of great mind and infinite humor, but that he despised the man on account of his ultra-toryism. It was a judgment that was not calculated to fan any incipient interest in the theater in a community that was still close to the frontier.

WHY DID CLEVELAND'S FIRST ATTEMPT TO HAVE A UNIVERSITY FAIL? — In the fall of 1850 Cleveland University had started the instruction of a small group of students in the Mechanics Block at Ontario and Prospect, probably chiefly for the accommodation of Oberlin students who were following the president in his Cleveland adventure.[6] However, others were there. Justus L. Cozad of East Cleveland was among them.[7] The formal opening took place April 2, 1851, but still in temporary quarters. The new building in University Heights was not ready. On August 31, 1851, commencement exercises ending the first term occurred. Three students, all from Oberlin College, received degrees from the new institution. A faculty of eight professors had been assembled. The president, Asa Mahan, a graduate of Hamilton College

6 For the beginnings of Cleveland University see Part II, Canal Days, p. 58.
7 Recollections of Justus L. Cozad, W. R. H. S. Mss. no. 526.

The Old Academy of Music. Built about 1852.

Case Hall. To be a Fanueil Hall for Cleveland. On site of present Federal Bldg.

and Andover Theological Seminary, was professor of mental and moral philosophy; John A. Nichols, a West Pointer, professor of mathematics; Carl Ruger, head of the department of modern languages. Dr. O. G. Amor was called from the University of Iowa as professor of natural science; and B. A. Norville was professor of music. One of the faculty had left his chair of rhetoric and belles lettres at Oberlin College to become head of the department of elocution, oratory and belles lettres in Cleveland University. Justus L. Cozad in his "Recollections" recalled a Plympton as professor of civil engineering and Arnold as professor of Latin. On March 17, 1852 the *Daily True Democrat* said the University then had a faculty of fourteen.

Early in 1852 the school moved to the new brick building in University Heights. Extend Ontario across the river to the Heights on the South side, and you have the location on University Avenue. Justus Cozad says that he then, with a classmate, went to board with Ahaz Merchant near the University. He gives the names of the following friends at the University: J. H. Maxon, Lewis Harrington, J. D. McKinney, Ed. Duty, Dan Duty and Newell Cozad, also two west side boys whom he identified as Dave and Prior. At the second commencement in June, 1852, eight received their degrees, five of whom had been students at Oberlin College before coming to Cleveland.

On August 20, 1851, the *Daily True Democrat* published an address by President Mahan before the National Educational Convention then meeting in Cleveland on the Character and Comparative Merits of the Old and the New Systems of Liberal Education. He claimed that two old institutions, Brown and the University of Virginia, and two new foundations, Rochester and Cleveland were based on a new system of liberal education — the freedom of the individual student to choose his courses, one or more, and pursue them until thoroughly mastered; to give individuals in fields like engineering, agriculture and the fine arts opportunities they could not enjoy under the rigidly

33

controlled, regimented systems of the time; to offer to the community opportunities to hear in public lectures the most recent results of departmental investigations.

In an editorial in the *Western Agriculturalist* Colonel Charles Whittlesey made the following significant statement: "With the exception of clergymen and those destined for literature, a long course in languages is certainly not indispensable. How often does a farmer, a mechanic, or even an attorney find it necessary to refer to his Latin? The Cleveland University proposes to make the studies of exact and natural sciences characteristic of the institution, and leave the subject of study open to the student or his guardians". That it was the introduction into the west of President Wayland's ideas, which had just been adopted at Brown University, was openly proclaimed. It pointed, a generation early, the way higher education in the United States was destined to go. In another respect the plan was unique for the time. It was to be a non-sectarian institution but to avoid the charges of the time against state universities by having various denominations represented in the departments of instruction.

Members of Cleveland University faculty were required to deliver courses of popular lectures on the principles and practical application of their subjects. In 1851 and 1852 public lectures were announced for Tuesday and Friday evenings by members of the faculty and visiting professors, carrying the influence of the university beyond its student body.

On the second commencement, June, 1852, the university reached its brightest days. Exercises were held in the university, in the park nearby and finally in Old Stone Church. The editors of the three daily newspapers gave the university liberal support. From outward appearances the third year opened in September under favorable circumstances. On August 7, 1852, the *Daily True Democrat* said, "The affairs of Cleveland University have been substantially arranged and placed on a sound and permanent basis." It must have been a shock to hear that beneath the surface all was not well. Some knew that Mrs. Brewster Pelton, one of the Oberlin supporters of President Mahan, had broken with him; that William Slade, former member of congress and governor of Vermont, and now a Cleveland lawyer and secretary and treasurer of the corporation, had resigned. But the climax in the rapidly sinking institution came with the resignation of President Mahan December 13, 1852.

In the following March Asa Mahan was elected president of the Homeopathic College of Cleveland. After that the newspapers ceased to mention Cleveland University. Apparently the institution dissolved in 1853. An effort was made to reorganize it, for the Directory of 1856 gives a list of new trustees and officers with Dudley Baldwin, president; Samuel Foljambe, secretary; Seth Chamberlain, Samuel Williamson, Etham Rogers, Jacob Perkins, William Herrick and John S. Newberry, trustees, but with the notation that the institution was "inoperative." The records are lost. Perhaps some family has these valuable papers. Such things do happen. The records of Willoughby University 1834-1847, have within this year (1945) finally come to the Historical Society for preservation and use.

Cleveland University disappeared and its building was taken over in 1859 by Humiston's Cleveland Institute. But why had it failed? Rochester University was based on the same general principles. Cleveland has liked to attribute the failure to the idiosyncrasies of Asa Mahan. These may easily have been a burden. The "new education" was a threat to the established order of church institutions of the Western Reserve — Oberlin and Western Reserve colleges, Baldwin and Hiram institutes. The old system was the one the college graduates of Cleveland knew and expected to benefit by. These factors were against Cleveland University. But in Rochester the people subscribed $150,000 for their university. Nothing of the kind happened in Cleveland. The land speculators, who, in the first instance launched the project to build up their holdings, were unable or unwilling to aid it in its extremities. Perhaps Cleveland was still too near the frontier for such an innovation to thrive.

THE SEMINARIES HAVE A SERIOUS RIVAL IN THE PUBLIC SCHOOLS—The Public School System steadily took over instruction in the lower grades, except in Catholic and German districts, where parochial or schools for German speaking children existed. In 1853 the office of superintendent of schools was created and Andrew Freese, who had been principal of the high school since 1846, was appointed to the place. Three years later a new high school building was dedicated. Located on the site of the Citizens Building, today, and designed by Heard and Porter, it was a brick building, faced with sandstone on the Euclid Street front. It was of "the Romanesque style of architecture," with turrets and portico of cut stone. In the decade of the 'fifties, however, it is obvious that the people had not yet come to appreciate the beneficence of the city fathers. In his Early History of the Cleveland Public Schools, Superintendent Freese reported that twenty-five percent of the scholars were absent each day.

Soon after the union of Ohio City and Cleveland a west side high school was established. For technical reasons only, it went by the name of Branch High School. In 1859 two evening schools had been organized, one on the east side, the other on the west. In the face of the aggressive leadership of the superintendent and the board of school managers, private schools and seminaries, the adventures of individual teachers had hard sledding. Gradually the fly-by-night schools disappeared from the announcements in the newspapers. Only the incorporated institutions with strong local support survived, and even they had their financial difficulties. Linda T. Guilford, *Story of a School*, gives the record. At the close of the 'fifties Miss Guilford's Academy at the "Point," Prospect and Huron Streets, passed through a succession of financial crises, but finally, located in a new home on the south side of Huron, near Euclid, found a place of great usefulness in the educational history of

Cleveland. Its graduates long remembered Miss Guilford's teaching and example and their school home, Cleveland Academy, the "Brick Academy."

In 1850 another stock company bought the old homestead of Moses Kelly, far out, two and one-eighth miles, in a rural, forested section of Kinsman (now Woodland) and built a three story brick building. They installed Dr. Samuel St. Johns, a professor in Western Reserve College and the Medical School, as principal, and a faculty that would have made any college faculty in the Western Reserve envious. In 1858 St. Johns went to a professorship in the College of Physicians and Surgeons, New York City. The seminary soon passed into other hands, its glorious days over, having barely escaped becoming a college by the weight and ambitions of its faculty. Humiston's so-called Cleveland Institute, Humiston's Institute for short, occupied the building abandoned by Cleveland University. It was a co-educational school. In spite of their financial difficulties, the faculties of these schools in the 'fifties, were larger than those of the public high schools and offered students richer programs of education.

At the opening of the decade Bishop Rappe purchased Judge Cowles' home on Euclid Street, where the Taylor Company is now located, and made it over into an academy, primarily for Catholic girls. Several Ursuline Sisters from France were brought to the school as teachers. It is quite evident that Cleveland families of comfortable means sent their girls to their own private schools, the boys to academies away from home.

CULTURE BY LECTURES AND BOOKS — The coming of the railroads was no less a stimulus for the intellectual life than for business. Ordinarily only those able to buy books or newspapers found the means to advance in general knowledge. Book dealers there were ready to help them. The City Directory of 1861 gave the names of ten such houses. One of them, at least, became an influence for good. In 1852 the book house of Moses C. Younglove & Company, famous throughout Canal Days, became J. B. Cobb and Company. His half-brother assistants had taken over. There was something logical about the succession. Father Cobb's interest in books and in ancient history in particular had exhibited itself in naming his progeny. It is impossible to resist the temptation to give his contribution to history, no small bit in more senses than one. Boys and girls, they bore the names Lucius Marcius, Marcius Lucius, Junius Brutus, and Lucia Marcia, Brutus Junius, Caius Cassius, Cassius Caius, and Marcia Lucia. And there the classical line ran out, or the father saw the end of his days approaching. The youngest was given a biblical name, Daniel, of course. At any rate the father's interest in books carried over. J. B. Cobb & Co. established a book store in Chicago, a branch of the Cleveland concern. Junius, Brutus and Caius became more than book merchants in Cleveland.

Since 1848 the Cleveland Library Association had become a fixed part of the cultural life of Cleveland. At the end of ten years its book collection numbered 3,000 volumes, and a membership of 500 subscribers broadening the basis for a cultured community. Libraries and book stores with their books on antiquity and the occult left a large public unsatisfied. Travel was a novelty few experienced. That left the lecture system of the day an important educational force for any part of the community which craved information. Several organizations, the Forest City Lyceum, the Young Men's Christian Association, the Young Men's Literary Association and the Library Association maintained annual lecture courses. Hardly a notable lecturer of the United States escaped the alluring offers of their officers. A list of the more prominent lecturers who came several times with their subjects reveals the intellectual curiosity of the time. Henry Ward Beecher came three times, speaking on such subjects as "The Ministration of the Beautiful," and "The Commonwealth"; George W. Curtiss, three times, "Democracy and Education" and "Education is the Best Policy"; Ralph Waldo Emerson, three times, "Culture", "The English Race" and "Rules of Success"; Edward Everett once, "Washington"; Horace Greeley twice, "Poets and Poetry"; Horace Mann, four times, "Man Above Brute and Man Below Brute;" Wendell Phillips, three times, "The Lost Arts," "Philosopher of Travel"; and Bayard Taylor, six times, "India", "Life in the North," "Humboldt", "Men, Custom and Climate."

Only one prominent lecturer of the period ventured into the slavery controversy. On March 1, 1860, Cassius M. Clay spoke on the "Causes of the Rise and Decline of this Nation." At the time when the nation was drifting fast toward Civil war over slavery the subjects of public lectures in Cleveland were generally innocuous, calculated by lecture committees to hurt no one's feelings.

When it came to commenting upon lecturers Artemus Ward's column in the *Plain Dealer* never pulled the punches. Horace Greeley's lecture brought the following: "a great many persons think he is a great man, and he rather inclines to that opinion himself . . . he wears cowhide brogans, and is eccentric. Success to him. Long may he wave." "His delivery is not simply bad, but positively diabolical." Of Emerson he said, "He is chock full of scholarship. He is stuffed with knowledge on all sorts of subjects. He is an *immense* man and we hope those who hear him tonight will understand him." After hearing him Ward wrote, "For our part we had as lief see a perpendicular coffin behind a lecture desk as Emerson." Bayard Taylor was apparently popular among Cleveland audiences. "The hall was literally packed full, every nook and corner." The fact that such a wide traveler could say that Cleveland was one of the most beautiful cities in the world helped, of course, but for that matter, perhaps he was right.

FAKIRS AND STAR-GAZERS BECOMING UNPOPULAR — Judging from the newspaper announcements of lecturers, Clevelanders were no longer primarily interested in hearing about monstrosities or watching the tricks of fakirs. "Phrenology" and "animal magnetism" were giving place to lectures on the mechanic arts, natural phenomena and animal life. Professor St. Johns of the Medical School and Colonel Charles Whittlesey were frequent speakers in the lecture series. It is clear that the intellectual level in Cleveland was rising. Several agencies were influential in the change. The Arkites had a wholesome general influence, the Medical School and the Academy of Science more direct, particularly in the cultivation of science.

THE ACADEMY OF NATURAL SCIENCE — Organized in 1845 by members of the faculty of the Medical School, represented by Kirtland, St. Johns and Cassels; by Arkites, represented by William Case, Rufus K. Winslow and Hamilton L. Smith, and by a few others with no such connections, Henry C. Kingsley, Judge Sherlock J. Andrews, Charles W. Heard, the architect, and William Beattie, the Academy of Natural Science in the 'fifties was Cleveland's most powerful cultural institution. It had a Museum of Natural History in the Medical School building, maintained an annual series of lectures in the field of scientific progress, and a publication, the *Annals of Science*, in which the results of their work appeared.[8] In addition Dr. Kirtland published a weekly journal, *The Family Visitor*. For the time *The Family Visitor* made an amazing record for scholarly interest and public spirit. Dr. Kirtland was a physician, geologist, horticulturist, botanist and zoologist, no mean authority in each and an inspiration to all associated with him.

The Museum of Natural History occupied a room on the second floor of the Medical School. The cases contained extensive scientific exhibits loaned for indefinite periods by the school, by Dr. Kirtland, Colonel Whittlesey and Rufus K. Winslow.[9] The Academy of Natural Science met ordinarily twice a month

[8] Proceedings of the Cleveland Academy of Natural Science, 1845-1859.

[9] The Historical Society has a manuscript account of the meetings of the Academy, Dec. 12, 1856 and July 4, 1858, together with a floor plan of the Museum and the description of the contents of the cases. Mss. no. 168.

and during the winter season on alternate weeks, between the meetings, maintained a series of public lectures upon some subject connected with natural science. The papers prepared by the members and read at the regular meetings were published in the *Annals*. Correspondence of Dr. Kirtland with Louis Agassiz, one of the greatest American scientists of the day, was also published in the *Proceedings* from time to time. It was intended that the *Annals of Science* should also serve as a record of the inventions and improvements in applied science. In the latter part of the 'fifties the proceedings were published in *The Ohio Farmer*, a Cleveland publication, the *Annals* having been suspended.

A POPULAR WEEKLY — THE FAMILY VISITOR — Dr. Kirtland's schemes for community advancement included a journal to popularize science. In the first number of *The Family Visitor*, Jan. 3, 1850, he wrote, "To the Public": Believing that the works of fiction which occupy so large a space in most of the so-called family papers of the present day tend to corrupt the heart and debase the mind; that the political press labors more for the voter than for the family circle, and the professionally religious, temperance and literary papers, from their exclusive character, are circumscribed in their circulation, it will be our object to present a sheet which, while it will in a degree partake of the character of these papers, will nevertheless be free from those features which limit their circulation and thus diminish their influence." He expressed the hope that their work might interest the whole family, instruct the mind and improve the heart. He promised that the organ would be non-partisan, not taking sides in politics or religious controversies, and provide information on the proceedings of Congress, foreign news, besides articles on natural science, agriculture and horticulture.

It tried various devices to live up to its ambitions to be a family paper. For a time there was a page for parents and children. It carried a course of instruction in agriculture and articles on agricultural chemistry. It also had a series of short articles on subjects of current interest; on rubbers, for example, for men and women; one on local natural history, "The Birds of Winter" and "Women's Place in Society." It published several scientific articles by Louis Agassiz, and sketches of famous men. Articles on education were frequent and commonly there was a page on religious subjects. The health of the community and methods for its preservation naturally found space in a journal edited by the foremost medical authority in Cleveland. "The Duration of Eternity" and the "Unity of the Human Race" were the subjects of two long articles. Its aims were high, perhaps too high, for a popular audience. The publication was moved to Hudson after a few years in Cleveland and was abandoned after eight years.[10]

THE FIRST HISTORICAL SOCIETY—As the decade advanced cultural interests seemed to broaden and gain in momentum. A half dozen monthly periodicals of one kind and another, scientific, literary, political or religious, were started, only to cease after a few issues. The starting of them indicated the larger expectations for the future, characteristic of life in the booming times of the new railroads, with the resulting expansion of industries and trade. There were those who thought of the difference between pioneer days and those in which they lived, and sought not only to know the record but to see that it was preserved.

In February 1858 the Cuyahoga County Historical Society was organized. Leonard Case, Sr. was chosen president, John Barr, Clerk of the Court of Common Pleas and the local historian of the day, became secretary, and Samuel Williamson, treasurer. Colonel Charles Whittlesey, Ahaz Merchant and George B. Merwin constituted a board of trustees. In order to make the organization county-wide, local committees, with a vice-president for each township, were created. Early settlers and township officers were given special privileges with the expectation that such persons could aid in the collection and preservation of historical material.[11]

10 The Historical Society has the complete file of *The Family Visitor*.
11 *Cleveland Daily Review*, Feb. 16, 1858; W. R. H. S. Tracts, no. 27, p. 5.

Full accounts of the Society's early activities were published in the newspapers. During 1858 the reports of the several township committees on local history were published in the *Cleveland Leader*, preserving information which would have disappeared with the passing of the early settlers. The Society held "grand county picnic pioneer celebrations" at Newburgh in June and October 1858 and June 1860. Like a county fair, public speaking and the exhibition of relics, instead of pigs, cattle and horses, marked the occasions. Writing of the meeting of 1860, the editor of the *Leader* said that "all had a grand time", 5,000 and more and that the "celebration had exceeded the previous ones in numbers, music, speeches, relics and enthusiasm." Artemus Ward gave over his local column in the *Plain Dealer* to a description of the meeting. He suppressed his sense of humor or skepticism, even when he described an old oaken chest which came over on the Mayflower.

The occasion appears to have been a "circus day" for the county, with main tent, stunts and side shows of curiosities and enormities, with a goodly amount of invaluable manuscripts and relics. The records of the Society were later turned over to the Western Reserve Historical Society. Several of the relics mentioned in the contemporary newspapers may now be seen at the Society's museum: for example, Rudolphus Edwards' compass used in 1798 in surveying the first road from the Pennsylvania line to Cleveland; the millstones of the first Newburgh flour mill, recently installed at the museum by the commissioners of Cuyahoga County; Allen Gaylord's painting, representing Cleveland in 1797, and Amos Spafford's map of the City of Cleveland in 1796. It is evident from Colonel Whittlesey's statement that he had already begun to accumulate the early surveys of the Western Reserve, and other manuscript material which he was ultimately to give to the Historical Society. Apparently the Samuel Huntington Correspondence which this Society now possesses came through the Cuyahoga County Historical

Society. Certainly the articles in the newspapers had stirred up interest in local history. A third picnic was planned for June, 1861, at Doan's Corners, East Cleveland, but the Cuyahoga County Historical Society became a casualty of the Civil War. Its program never passed beyond the gathering stage. Its business meetings were usually held in the county court house.

IN ALL THIS AND MORE THE EDITORS HAVE A PART — In 1850 there were three daily newspapers and two weeklies; ten years later the number was five dailies and four weeklies, not to include several short lived papers. The *Daily True Democrat* changed its name to become the *Cleveland Leader*. In 1852 Joseph and James C. Medill with Edwin Cowles had established the *Forest City*, and a year later the *True Democrat* and the *Forest City* took the name the *Forest City Democrat* and in 1854 the *Morning Leader*. Shortly afterwards Joseph Medill went to Chicago to take over the *Chicago Tribune*. The editorial management of the *Leader* changed several times in the decade, but before the end Edwin Cowles began his long career at its head. These papers all began as free soil advocates, freedom of all federal territories from slavery, and with the establishment of the Republican party, Cowles led his paper into its fold. He found great satisfaction in castigating the Democratic Party on the slavery issue. The Historical Society's file of the *True Democrat*, *Forest City* and *Leader* is nearly complete, together covering the years 1847 to 1917.

By 1860 the *Cleveland Herald* and the *Plain Dealer* were well established newspapers, the former nearly forty years old, the latter nearly half of that. For most of the time W. J. Gray of the *Plain Dealer* and Joseph A. Harris of the *Herald* were local editors and political leaders of great power, the former in the Democratic Party, while Harris was following the Whigs into the Republican Party. In 1857 George A. Benedict succeeded Harris at the helm of the *Herald*. The Historical Society has an almost complete file of both papers.

At the close of the 'fifties two morning newspapers, the *Daily Review*, established in 1857, neutral in politics, H. N. Johnson, editor, and the *National Democrat*, 1859, Democratic in party politics, C. B. Flood, editor, were struggling to make a place for themselves amid the party confusion just preceding the Civil War. Flood's paper was established to harass the *Plain Dealer* for opposing Buchanan's administration. The *Daily Review* broke into the field as a penny paper, the first in Cleveland. In April, 1858, it also began the publication of a Sunday edition. The contemporary opposition to such a desecration of the Sabbath was apparently too much, for only eleven issues were attempted. The *Review* was heavily laden with religious and moral subjects, but carried a weekly review of current events — "Noticeable Events," and a column on "Wit and Humor". Both newspapers were casualties of the Civil War. The Historical Society has a complete file of the *Review*, five issues of the *Daily National Democrat* and a complete file of the weekly edition.

It didn't take a Civil War to limit the life time of the *Cleveland Daily Express* or the *Daily Clevelander*, or the *Daily Dispatch*. None of them survived more than a few months. So many journalistic enterprises reflected the large expectations, intellectual ferment, and free enterprise of the 'fifties. The *Dispatch* lasted for four months, the *Express* and *Clevelander* a little more than a year. The Society's file of the last two is almost complete, but no copies of the *Dispatch* seem to have survived.

There were several weeklies. The *Ohio Farmer*, started in 1852, a journal for farmers' families entered upon a long and successful career, quite alone in its field. The Society's file is complete from 1852 to 1942. Almost as much might be said for the *Ohio Cultivator*, founded in 1845 and published until 1859, and of this the Society has a complete file.

For a short time the German speaking population had two weekly newspapers, *Germania*, founded in 1846, and *Waechter am Erie*, in 1852. The first espoused at the beginning the cause of the Democratic Party, the latter the Whig, and later the Republican Party. Both of them also published a semi-weekly edition in their good years. For a short while the Germans in Cleveland also published a newspaper in English, the *Cleveland Journal*. The Society has an almost complete file of *Waechter am Erie*, a few scattered numbers of the *Germania*, but none of the *Journal*.

The number of weeklies started, only to fail after a few issues, is quite a commentary on the working of free enterprise in the newspaper field in the 'fifties. Type setters, reporters, and assistant editors tried to advance into the coveted position of editor-in-chief. A list of these short lived newspapers is given below with a statement of what the Society possesses. It is hoped that some of these may still be found in old piles of family papers, and given to the Historical Society.[12]

[12]   *Short Lived Weeklies of the 'Fifties*

Name	Editor	Years Published	Comments
The Am. Advertiser	H. M. Addison	1850	Died within a year. Neutral in politics. The Society has two issues.
The Aliened American		1853	The Society possesses one copy, April 9, 1853.
The American Eagle		1854, 1857	Copies for Aug. 5, 1854, Aug. and Sept., 1857. Devoted to lotteries.
Buckeye Democrat	S. Ward Smith	1857-1858	No copies are known to have survived.
Cleveland Commercial	T. B. and L. G. Hine	1851-1853	A family and business journal, "advocating morality, education, temperance, and equal rights for all mankind," but what editor would have denied such a platform. The Society has copies for Nov., 1851, Oct. 13, 20, 27, Nov. 3, 1853.
Cleveland Commercial Gazette	S. S. Barry John F. Laws	1856-1868	Published by the leaders devoted to the market and commercial news. The Society has two issues, Mar. 28, April 11, 1861.

CULTURAL DEVELOPMENTS DURING THE 'FIFTIES

AND THEN ARTEMUS WARD STEALS THE SHOW—No account of the part the newspapers had in the cultural history of Cleveland before the Civil War or of their importance as a source of history would be complete without an account of the part of the most interesting editorial writer of the period. In October, 1857, Charles Farrar Browne, joined the *Plain Dealer* as associate editor, serving in fact in a triple role, as an associate for Gray, needed for much of the time because of Gray's illness, and as local and commercial editor as well, all at ten dollars a week. His local column on "City Facts and Fancies" became a colorful feature. The account of a local thief's performances would make the readers eager for another story of the kind even at the expense of some victim.

Name	Editor	Years Published	Comments
Dodge's Literary Museum	Orsian E. Dodge	1857-60	No copies known to exist.
The Harpoon	H. M. Addison	1852-1853	A temperance paper "to be continued 'til the enactment of the Maine law in Ohio." Society has a file from April to Oct., 1853.
The Illuminate		1857	The Society has the first issue, Nov. 14, 1857.
The Independent		1857	No issues known to exist.
Old Soldiers' Advocate	Col. G. F. Lewis	1859-1876	Society's file, 1859-1864.
Peoples' Record	W. H. Day	1856	None known to exist.
The Rescuer		1859	Published at the county jail. It was an organ of the radical anti-slavery group which appealed from the federal law providing for the return of fugitive slaves to the Higher Law and the Underground Railroad. Society has first issue, July 4, 1859.
Scott's Soup Bowl		1852	The Society has the issue of July 15, 1852.
The Spie (sometimes-Spy)		1858	A Democratic newspaper. The issue the Society possesses, Jan. 2, 1858.

In his column of January 30, 1858, appeared for the first time an humorous article describing a side show in Pittsburgh that the proprietor, Artemus Ward, wanted to bring to Cleveland.

Pittsburgh, Jan. the 27th, 1858

To the Plane Deeler Sir i write to no how about the show bisness in Cleeveland i have a show consisting in part of a Calforny Bare two snakes tame foxies &c also wax works my wax works is hard to beat, all say they is life like and nateral curiosities among my wax works is Our Saveyer Gen taylor and Dokter Webster in the ackt of killing Parkman. now Mr. Editor scratch off few lines and tel me how is the show bisness in your good city i shall have hanbills printed at your offis you scratch my back & i will scratch your back, also git up a grate blow in the paper about my show dont forget the wax works. Yours truly,

Artemus Ward
Pitsburg, Penny.

P.S. Pitsburg is a i horse town A.W.

Name	Editor	Years Published	Comments
Spirit of the Lakes	Rev. R. H. Leonard	1850	Published by the Western Seamen's Friendly Society. None known to have survived.
The Spiritual Universe	L. I. Everett	1854-1860	The Society possesses scattered issues of 1854, 1855 and 1856.
The Vanguard	Wm. Denton, Alfred Cridge and his wife, Anna Denton Cridge.	1859-1860	The Society possesses one issue, May 28, 1859.
The Western Weekly Gleaner		1859	The Society's file contains issues for July 17, Aug. 6, and Dec. 2, 1859.
The Workingclass Union		1858	The Society possesses the issue of Aug. 28, 1858.

The editor adds —

"We believe Mr. W. would do well with his show here,
and advise him to come along immediately."

Similar letters were published from time to time, just frequently
enough to keep the readers in a state of expectancy, with the
showman travelling among Ohio towns, always on the brink
of getting to Cleveland. Signed Artemus Ward, they gave editor
Browne a pen-name. But Browne's repertoire was not limited
to the record of a travelling showman. There was a young man,
George Blair, "A prepossessing young man with an annual
income of $2500", seeking a wife by correspondence. Browne's
column from time to time published letters with comments on the
merits of each one of the applicants, a fill in between the Artemus
Ward letters. Patent medicines gave him frequent opportunities —
a "tremendous medicine, Dr. Boogles Double Refined All-Healing
Vegetable Pills — joy to the afflicted."

He found a place for amusing reminiscences of life in Toledo.
The appearance of a red petticoat in the street one cold day
attracted his attention and made him want to see more of them.
He didn't seem to take the politicians very seriously. On the eve
of an election he came out with what purported to be "Political
Sermon by the Rev. Hardshell Pike," announcing, "My Brethren,
S. A. Douglas is my candidate and Mrs. S. A. Douglas is my can-
didatess." In July, 1859, Artemus Ward left the show business
long enough to deliver an oration on the Fourth of July in
Wethersfield, Connecticut. It was one of his best interpretations
of the average political oration of the day. He introduced comic
woodcuts by George Hoit to illustrate his articles.

Extravagances were a part of his stock in trade. There was the
story of the lion that jumped against a pole with such force
that he was split from head to tail. The owner put him together,
and it worked. The lion lived, but the halves were put together
t'other end to! He did more than entertain his readers. His local
column became at times that of the dramatic or music critic.

Music and the theater found thorough and sympathetic reviews in "City Facts and Fancies".

At the end of three years in Cleveland, November, 1860, Charles Farrar Browne left the *Plain Dealer* for New York City. He had outgrown the local environment of a small city daily with its endless details of reporting, and particularly the second place he occupied. He had learned of a wider market for his humorous stories. He left Cleveland to become a member of the staff of *Vanity Fair*, established in New York City to rival the London *Punch*, and from that point of advantage passed on to become a national figure on the lecture platform. The Historical Society possesses two bits of evidence of his Cleveland days, the chair and table which he used in his *Plain Dealer* office.

VII. THE COMING OF THE CIVIL WAR

THE IRREPRESSIBLE ISSUE—Through the 'fifties Cleveland had made progress in many ways. All evidence pointed to continuing advancement. The Secession of South Carolina and its sister states in the winter of 1860-1861 came as a tremendous shock to a complacent people, whether in Cleveland or elsewhere. For a full generation the disputes over slavery in the states and the territories had muddied politics. Again and again statesmen had postponed and compromised and hoped. Every political issue had sooner or later turned to ashes under the blighting influence of its bearing on the institution of the Southland. Churches had divided, North and South. Political propaganda — pro-slavery or anti-slavery — had come to divide the nation spiritually.

ANTI-SLAVERY IN THE WESTERN RESERVE — In the Western Reserve as a whole, outside of Cleveland, the population was predominantly of New England origin and profoundly affected by the Garrisonian movement for immediate, uncompensated emancipation. The colleges at Oberlin, Hudson, Berea and Hiram were centers of abolitionism, the extreme form of anti-slavery. It need hardly be said that anti-slavery in its milder form was well-nigh universal. Even the majority of the South would have claimed to be anti-slavery. In the whole South owners of slaves constituted only twenty-five per cent of the population. It was the social problem arising from the presence of a large mass of freedmen that alarmed the poor whites even more than it did the owners and complicated every move toward freeing the slaves. It was the way out that puzzled the poor whites as well as the planters.

In Cleveland there was a tendency to try to avoid rocking the boat, a tendency which made its Western Reserve neighbors brand it as conservative. On the slave issue the ministers and editors of Cleveland, the chief agencies in the formation of public opinion, were conservative, that is, not Garrisonian abolitionists. The constitution of the Cleveland Anti-Slavery Society declared that it would endeavor to accomplish its object, not by encouraging the oppressed to resort to physical force, but by enlightening the public mind in regard to the true character of slavery, by setting before the slave holders of the community at large the justice, safety and necessity of immediately emancipating all slaves, and restoring their right to all the people of color and especially encouraging the education and the industry of the free colored people of the country.

Although the constitution bears no date, it was apparently organized in 1837 in Old Stone Church. The list of signers (132) includes the names of Dr. Samuel C. Aiken, Sherlock J. Andrews, S. L. and J. L. and Mary H. Severance, and William Williams, all of the Old Stone Church, the one church under the charge of some of its members for conservatism on slavery. At the same time there was a county society with Edward Wade, President, and T. C. Severance, secretary.[13] However, it is significant that the Cleveland Directories after 1837 did not include an anti-slavery society in their list of societies, and that between 1840

13 W. R. H. S. Mss. no. 1407.

and 1861 the *Cleveland Newspaper Digest* mentions a meeting of one of these organizations only twice, once in 1841 and once in 1859. In neither case did the meeting have more than a brief statement in the newspapers. Even the Oberlin-Wellington rescue case of 1859, where some thirty-seven Oberlinites took the law into their own hands and rescued a fugitive slave from his captors and found themselves in jail in Cleveland, at the mercy of the Federal Court, stirred up the anti-slavery elements outside of Cuyahoga County more than within. The newspaper accounts of the mass meeting in Cleveland, May 24, 1859, leave no doubt that the local leaders of public opinion were holding aloof, and that it was dominated by the radical elements of the rural areas of the Western Reserve. Joshua A. Giddings was the presiding genius, and source of inspiration. It would seem that the radical abolitionist chilled the fervor of the Cleveland anti-slavery societies. In a sermon, December 16, 1851, Dr. Aiken said, "No good cause was ever more wretchedly managed than the cause of anti-slavery has been in the United States."

THE CONSERVATIVES IN CLEVELAND KEPT IN HOT WATER — In August, 1857, a convention of the friends of compensated emancipation was held in Cleveland, a national affair. Some thought to buy the slaves with the proceeds from public land sales, others thought other federal sources of revenue would be available. They accepted the view that slavery was national, not sectional. They set the rate of compensation at $250 for each slave. It was a movement that died at birth, but worthy of a larger hearing.

Dr. Aiken of Old Stone Church found a middle-of-the-road course difficult. His abolitionist members "insisted that he devote his pulpit utterances wholly to their burning issue." In his sermon for June 3, 1860, Dr. Aiken said: "There are some things which I cannot pass over in silence . . . the ultra reforms which have been discussed, upon Temperance, Slavery, etc., have rendered it extremely difficult for the pastor to maintain order and harmony in his church." There was division within the churches, the ministers differed among themselves.

In the election of 1860, the editors were sharply divided on the slavery issue. Charles B. Flood of the *Daily National Democrat* supported the extreme Southern group and its candidate, Senator Breckinridge. Gray of the *Plain Dealer*, to a slight degree anti-slavery, followed the leadership of Stephen A. Douglas. The *Herald* and the *Leader*, of course, supported Lincoln, but the *Leader* tended to be the more critical of the South. At the polls in November the people of Cuyahoga County voted overwhelmingly for Lincoln, giving him nearly twice the combined vote of his three opponents. It was distinctly an anti-slavery vote, but in no sense a commitment to unconditional emancipation. The Republican platform only committed its followers on one slavery issue — that was that the "normal condition of all the territory of the United States is that of freedmen."

LINCOLN TRIED IN VAIN TO APPEASE THE SECEDERS—In the face of the secession of the cotton growing states, the President elect made it clear that he had no plan looking to an attack on slavery in the states. Indeed, he endorsed a projected constitutional amendment denying Congress any power to interfere with slavery in a state. As for the fugitive slave law and the underground railroad activities at the North, one of the sources of aggravation at the South, he promised, if the fugitive slave law were modified in certain offensive particulars, to see that it was enforced. It is now also clear that he was ready to abandon the territorial issue upon which his party was founded in 1854, since with the admission of Kansas in January, 1861, it was a dead issue. Except for the District of Columbia, the status of all federal territory with regard to slavery was determined by a law of Congress or by the laws of nature in favor of the North. By 1861, Kansas having been admitted into the Union, the Free Soil movement on which the Republican Party was primarily based was an abstract question. Slavery certainly could never secure a foothold in the territories. The times called for a constructive program of social reform which should extinguish slavery in the states, a matter no one advocated. Under the stress of impending war Lincoln considered withdrawing the federal troops from Fort Sumter if Virginia would dissolve its convention in Richmond, threatening secession. In the light of recent research, it can no longer be said that Lincoln in 1861 stood like a rock against compromise. Such was Lincoln's confidence in time and tide to settle this particular issue. Conservative that he was, he assumed that the next generation would extinguish slavery by peaceful means.

AN APPEAL TO FORCE TO ESTABLISH A NEW WHITE REPUBLIC — Appeasement came too late, too late and too little, though Lincoln could not have conceded more and held his party together. Propaganda, North and South, had done its work, fatally dividing the nation. In the winter of 1860-1861 there was nothing for Southern Leaders but to accept peaceful solutions as offered by the President elect or to make a war. And to make their answer clear they attacked the federal forces at Fort Sumter. The Southern forces had crossed the Rubicon.

THE NATIONAL SIN — The worst that can be said for the position of the South is that its people, planter and commoner, were confused by race prejudices and the complicated social and labor problems involved in the removal of the discipline of slavery. The Northern charge so loudly proclaimed by the abolitionists that slavery existed because of the criminality of the southern owners enraged them, and made any solution difficult. The worst that can be said of the northerners is that they exaggerated the evils of the slave system and disregarded the evils of the free labor system, and were totally ignorant of the complicated social problems they sought to solve. Slavery was a malignant growth for which all Americans were responsible. The sin was national in origin, not sectional. Some, particularly the southerners had sought to exploit their resources in land by slave labor, others, particularly the northern merchants, had maintained the slave trade, and so slavery had grown to be the national problem that it was. The burden of the solution, if it were to be a peaceful one, would have to be national. Inability to see that and act upon it was the great mistake of American statesmanship in the years before the war.

It was with saddened hearts that the country faced a Civil War. For the thoughtful men of the Western Reserve, Jacob D. Cox expressed their view — "With most of us the gloomy thoughts that a Civil War had begun in our own land overshadowed everything and seemed too great a price to pay for any good; a scourge to be borne only in preference to yielding the very groundwork of our republicanism."

In Cleveland the out and out pro-Southern dailies, the *National Democrat* and the *Daily Review*, gave up the ghost early in 1861. Their very existence for the time is a cause of wonderment, both democratic papers dividing the field with the *Plain Dealer*. For the three dailies that survived the crisis of the spring of 1861, the period meant a rapid increase in their circulation, doubling it. On April 22, the *Herald* announced that its circulation had increased the past week from 5,000 copies daily to 10,000. In June the *Herald* and the *Leader* began to publish both morning and afternoon issues. The *Plain Dealer* promised extra editions, "morning, noon, and night or as often as any additional news of importance" was received.

It is equally significant that the Democrats, Bell and Douglas followers, joined with the Republicans of Cleveland in April, 1861, to elect a union slate of municipal officers. Under the stress of the times, conservative men of all parties learned to vote together. In Ohio as in the South radical party men were pushed aside.

VIII. THE CIVIL WAR

THE ALARM. MINUTE GUARDS COME TO CLEVELAND — Once only during the Civil War were Union men in Cleveland much alarmed. During 1863 the growing secret organizations in the

Northwest, Knights of the Golden Circle, men weary of the war, ready for peace at any price, copperheads, southern sympathizers, brought about counter organizations of Union Leagues, pledged to unconditional loyalty to the government. In Cleveland each ward had its Union League, and a central committee for the city. On March 31, 1863, these held a mass meeting at Brainard's Hall. In July they resorted to the Minute Guards, so-called in memory of the Revolutionary Minute Men, defensive measures. The opponents of the war were united on Clement L. Vallandigham as candidate for Governor of Ohio. In October just before the election, the Republicans of Cuyahoga County hastily took a secret canvass of the voters, an approach to the modern straw voting. But there was really no cause for alarm in northern Ohio. The tide had turned with Vicksburg and Gettysburg. Vallandigham voters in the county tallied in the trial vote at less than 20 per cent, and still less in the fall election. In Ohio about one third of the voters expressed themselves in favor of peace at any price. If not alarming, in all its implications it was an astonishing mid-war expression of opinion.

INFLATION COMES WITH THE WAR — And so for four years the national pattern, war with all its consequences, marching and fighting, financial problems, public and private, prevailed. Local history was shaped by events which occurred far away. Cleveland, of course, was no exception. Thousands of young men left, in about the same proportions as elsewhere, for service as volunteers or as draftees. In a country unprepared for war, supplies and arms became hectic problems in every community. Without financial reserves and with a tax system geared for peace times, the Government found it difficult to meet the huge costs of war. Specie payments were suspended almost at once to protect the banks from demands for gold and silver which they could not have met. When it became evident that borrowing money from the citizenry would be a slow process, greenbacks, that is unsecured treasury notes, were resorted to by the United States as in the American revolution. Whether because of the want of confidence in the military leaders or in the methods of financing the war or because of the scarcity of supplies, probably for all three reasons, prices rose rapidly, more rapidly than salaries and wages, with great hardships for laborers and salaried classes in particular. Within a year the *Cleveland Leader* complained "that one year ago a bushel of corn would buy two pounds of coffee. Now it takes at least a bushel and a half to buy one pound of coffee." By 1864 prices had risen nearly 100 per cent, wages less than 50 per cent.

INDUSTRIAL EXPANSION FOR WAR — As hard money disappeared, small change became scarce, and the very scarcity became a barrier to ordinary business transactions. As in the Panic of 1837 local parties resorted to various devices for money — encased postage stamps (a simple way of using postage stamps as change), private token pieces (little copper coins, so to speak, issued by private individuals or companies) and shinplasters, (paper money in small denominations). Nevertheless the demand for goods, and particularly for war supplies, and the necessity under which the Government was to pay high prices to get results produced an industrial expansion. For Cleveland the chief expansion was the manufacture of iron products. In 1865 the Board of Trade reported that there were then two blast furnaces, six rolling mills, two forges, eight foundries, three spike, nail, rivet, nut and washer factories, employing altogether 3000 hands. In order to accomplish these things the receipts of coal and Michigan iron ore more than doubled during the Civil War. Among other developments Cleveland had become the chief ship building center of the Great Lakes. Wooden vessels they were, everyone, the result of the proximity of the fine timbers of Michigan and Canada.

THE NEW BUSINESS OF WAR TIMES — Cleveland had also fallen heir to a new industry. By the end of the war there were thirty oil refineries, making Cleveland the chief city in the production of "coal oil". A young man with little capital and half a dozen laborers could start a refinery. Coal oil sold for ten dollars a barrel. For coal, oil and iron ore Cleveland had become an important shipping center. Business expansion during the war extended into every field of manufacture and trade. New business houses were started, some of which have held a continuous history until the present day. There was, for example, the Higbee Company, 1860; the Weideman Company, 1861; the Stearn Company, the Leisy Brewing Company and the Lake Shore Saw Mill and Lumber Company, 1862; the Stone Shoe Company, 1863; Taylor and Boggis Foundry Company and the Neal Storage Company, 1864; and the Lake Erie Provision Company, the Wagner Awning Company and the White Manufacturing Company, the parent of both the White Sewing Machine Company and the White Motor Company, 1865.

With the coming of the Civil War it soon became apparent that the new transportation system had come in the nick of time. It would hardly be too much to say that the railroads saved the Union. They meant much for Cleveland as a factor in supplying its raw materials and also in marketing its war products. Supplying railroads with iron rails, passenger and freight cars was no small part of the increased industrial activity which marked the war time in Cleveland. Just as the year 1863 closed, the Atlantic and Great Western Railroad (Erie) was completed into Cleveland. Cleveland newspapers reported the arrival of "a train direct from New York on a track of six feet gauge." It was an event of double significance — a new route to the East and one that touched the oil fields in Pennsylvania. Its unusual width only emphasized the fact that the railroads had as yet not a uniform gauge, whereby freight cars could be moved from one road to another. Some railroads met the requirements of the time by a third rail. Much was done during the Civil War toward standardizing the gauge of railroads.

MONEY AND BANKING DURING THE WAR —All these changes called for expanded services by the Cleveland banks. On April 1, 1863, the *Cleveland Leader* observed that "one of the most remarkable features of these times is the steady and rapid accumulation of savings deposits", the outcome of higher wages as the war progressed and soldiers' bounties and wages, combined with local habits of thrift. During the war bank capital as a whole trebled. The City Bank of Cleveland paid its stockholders eight per cent in 1862, ten per cent in 1863 and 1864, an evidence of a profitable period.

THE NATIONAL BANK ACT — As often happens, problems of the war gave shape to banking history for the long period of peace to follow. The National Bank Act was given form in the darkest days of the Civil War; when money requirements were tremendous and the military situation still serious for the Union armies; when the fast declining value of Greenbacks threatened uncontrolled inflation like that which followed the issue of continental dollars during the American Revolution. The title of the Act tells the story of the financial objectives. It was "an Act to provide a National Currency, secured by a Pledge of United States Bonds, and to provide for the Circulation and Redemption thereof".

The new national banks were required to purchase bonds up to one third of their capital stock, and to deposit such bonds with the Treasury as security for a new system of national currency to be sponsored by such banks. It produced at once a market for United States bonds and a sound national currency. It was a war measure, cleverly conceived, but, as time would show, not well adapted to the monetary requirements of peace times. As the measure carried with it the power to tax state bank notes, the Ohio State Banking System with its Branch Banks fell with the passage of the National Bank Act. A national paper currency superseded all state systems, bringing the currency situation back to that before Jackson's famous veto message, but, be it noted, on a new basis. In place of the Bank of the United States with its several branches exercising the powers of banking and monetary control, the Civil War measure installed hundreds of local national banks, subjected to loose supervisory controls of the Treasury Department.

State banks might have continued under state charters, though they would lose whatever benefits there might have been in the privilege of sharing in state bank note issues. In Cleveland there was a rush to climb aboard the new national band wagon, in order to enjoy the anticipated advantages of national patronage. A group of business men with George Worthington as their President promptly organized the First National Bank. Another group with Joseph Perkins at the head organized the Second National Bank. The two Branch Banks of the State of Ohio disappeared as such. The Bank of Commerce was reorganized as the Commercial National Bank, and at the same time absorbed the Commercial Branch Bank, the charter of which would have expired in a few months. William A. Otis was the President of the combined institution. The Merchants Branch Bank became the Merchants National Bank with T. P. Handy as President. The City Bank waited until 1865, the year in which its first charter would expire, before adjusting itself to changing conditions as the National City Bank. In the same year the Society for Savings began to build on the Public Square, a building completed two years later.

IX. CULTURAL INSTITUTIONS DURING THE CIVIL WAR

WAR DIVERTS SUPPORT FROM CULTURAL THINGS — War makes hard times for cultural institutions in general, and the Civil War was no exception. Rising prices, the demand of the harassed government for increased taxes and bond subscriptions, and the uncertainties of business conditions — all combined to restrict the support of cultural agencies. Again and again Union forces barely avoided disaster. Foreign intervention was a menace throughout the early years of the War, from France in particular. Four years of hating, ravaging and killing are a strain on any people. Men fell, their bones to bleach in the sun, a ghastly sight. The public read with horror of Fredericksburg, Chancellorsville, and Gettysburg where Americans fell by ten thousands. One woman, who might have been from the North or South, wrote of how women felt during these times — "It seems we are never out of the sound of the Dead March of Saul. It comes, it comes until I feel inclined to close my ears and scream."

CASUALTIES OF THE CIVIL WAR — Colleges around Cleveland barely avoided the necessity of closing up entirely. Their men, faculty and students, went into military service, volunteers in large numbers. In June 1862 Western Reserve College postponed commencement exercises until October because a large part of the students had left. In the Medical School in Cleveland the attendance fell off seventy-five percent. (From 80 to 20). The efforts to establish a Cleveland University were abandoned. The Academy of Natural Science and its publications together with the Cuyahoga Historical Society were victims of shifts in interest and compelling war demands. Only the strong newspapers and literary publications survived. Promoters of literary enterprises found conditions unfavorable. In the newspapers war news claimed the bulk of the space. The *Plain Dealer* was nearly a casualty, not so much of the war as of the death of Gray and the policy of his successor who followed the cue of the copperheads, insisting that the war was a failure and Lincoln unfit. In 1863 the *Plain Dealer* supported Clement L. Vallandigham for governor and the following year General McClellan for president. (Gray, who died March 26, 1862, had supported Lincoln and the Union cause). The change in policy of the *Plain Dealer* antagonized the community with the result that its patronage steadily declined. In March 1865, publication of the paper was suspended, and the *Plain Dealer* seemed to have reached the end of its career, a victim of a confusion in editorial policy during a great Civil War. Seven weeks later the War practically over, under the auspices of a new editor, William W. Armstrong, the *Plain Dealer* had a fresh start.

WHAT HAPPENED TO THE FINE ARTS — The Cleveland Library Association maintained its lecture series throughout the war, only shortened. Under its auspices such popular lecturers as Bayard Taylor, Ralph Waldo Emerson, Edward Everett and Louis Agassiz came to Cleveland one or more times. In 1865 Artemus Ward came for a lecture on "Among the Mormons." May be this was the one for which he received a bill from a young lady for twenty-four buttons, so many hooks and eyes and other fixtures which she had broken on attending his lecture. The death of the President of the Cleveland Library Association, William Case, in 1862, was a serious blow for the Association and cultural movements of all kinds. Art and architects seemed to suffer severely under war conditions. The newspapers carried little information regarding art and the work of the artists. However, the homes of James Farmer, William J. Boardman, Samuel Livingston Mather and Henry Chisholm, all built during the Civil War, were in the classical style, fine examples of the best work of contemporary architects.

JOHN ELLSLER RETURNS — On the anniversary of the Battle of Lexington, 1862, John Ellsler returned to the Academy of Music as manager and shortly afterwards his stock company returned from a tour. From that time on through his managerial ability, music and the drama seemed anything but dormant. Each season found him busy with varied bookings, though not always profitable ones. Each year the Italian Grand Opera Company came to the Academy of Music for a few nights of Grand Opera. The Cleveland Musical Society seems to have been a casualty of the war, for it is not mentioned in the newspaper announcements. In 1862 the Zion Musical Society offered a short season of concerts.

Ellsler's promotional skill was confined mostly to theatricals.

Each year he gave Clevelanders an extensive and varied dramatic program. In many plays he or Mrs. Ellsler had a part. In July and November, 1863, he brought J. Wilkes Booth to the Academy for several nights in such plays as Richard III, Hamlet, Schiller's "Robbers" and Bulver's comedy, "Money." In his Memories Ellsler says that he had known him as a school boy in Baltimore, and had considered him as a Union man, and that in fact Booth in the spring of 1861 had been run out of Montgomery, Alabama, because of his utterances in behalf of the Union. Ellsler and Booth invested jointly in Pennsylvania oil properties during the Civil War.[14] Edwin Adams was the popular actor in Cleveland in the 'sixties, especially in Shakespearian plays. Both Mr. and Mrs. Ellsler had parts with him on several occasions.

THE RISE OF SPORTS AND GAMES — Horse-racing, cricket and curling seemed to be the chief sports. Outdoor skating and sleighing in season. But games and sports had relatively little space in the newspapers. To be sure, several times the editor of the *Cleveland Leader* took up the cudgels for them. "Let us, as a people, encourage athletic games and sports. We should have bathing houses on the lake shore and encourage women and girls to swim." He also noticed that baseball was becoming a national sport. In the latter years of the Civil War Cleveland had its own club and engaged in contests with teams of the surrounding cities. In September, 1865, the Forest City Club was organized.

SOLDIERS' AID SOCIETIES — Cultural activities and sports were forced to take second place, when it came to the requirements of a great war. Within a week after President Lincoln's first call for troops to preserve the Union the women of Cleveland had organized a Soldiers' Aid Society. Mrs. Benjamin Rouse was the President, Mary Clark Brayton, Secretary, and Ellen F. Terry, Treasurer. In October the Society became a branch of the United

14 W. R. H. S. Mss. no. 3025, pp. 133-5.

States Sanitary Commission. Dr. John S. Newberry, formerly of the Medical School Faculty, was Secretary of the Western Department of the Sanitary Commission. The women collected clothing, blankets and other supplies for the comfort of soldiers wherever there was a need, opened a soup house in Merwin Street, and became, in effect, a sewing circle to make articles for the soldiers and promoted the raising of vegetables. Farmers of the neighborhood to cooperate set aside the "soldiers' acre," humorously called the children's "Onion League." The *Cleveland Leader* gave them two columns for their use. As a matter of course the women had a large part in the care of the soldiers in the army hospitals in Cleveland, temporary structures, supplying comforts and care that eased the burden of the war for the unfortunates.

The Soldiers' Aid Society mobilized the women of Cleveland for a grand Sanitary Fair in February and March, 1864. The temporary building in the form of a Greek cross was erected at the center of the Public Square, really a group of halls. In the center was a Floral Hall, octagon in shape. On the west was the Ladies' Bazaar, the east an assembly room, the south the Hall of Machinery, Manufactures and Produce, and the north a Dining Hall. In addition war relics from battlefields were on exhibition. The "Ladies" published a daily "Sanitary Fair Gazette." The object was to raise funds for the Soldiers' Aid and the financial result seemed to contemporaries quite handsome.[15] Soldiers' Aid Societies and Sanitary Fairs were the order of the day. The surrounding counties of the Western Reserve had their Societies linked with the Cleveland Society and all large cities had Sanitary Fairs. Another organization, the Christian Commission, was formed early in the war, nation wide, to supply the soldiers with Bibles, books, magazines, and other reading matter. There was a branch in Cleveland. Most of its support came from contributions from the churches.

15 Mary Clark Brayton and Ellen F. Terry, "Our Acre and its Harvest".

CULTURAL INSTITUTIONS

THE COST OF A CIVIL WAR — The war ended at last, a long four years of civil strife for the Americans, and with it slavery as a legal institution fell. Even with a drawn peace in 1865 slavery must have gone, for it had largely disintegrated during the war. But war proved a costly way to solve an economic and social problem. In order to settle the issue statesmen had evaded, muddled and at long last left to younger men to fight out more than six hundred thousand gave their lives and other hundreds of thousands bore more or less grievous wounds and broken health through life. To end the wearisome conflict generals had devised a total war and scorched earth policy, bringing home to civilians — men, women, and children, as well as the military, the cold realities of modern warfare. Fields and factories, livestock and homes, whole cities had been destroyed. At one small town in Georgia the cotton factory was burned and four hundred young women operators were transported far behind the Union lines to make certain production would not be resumed. The Shenandoah, Georgia and South Carolina felt the effects of total destruction. Plantation homes, cities — Atlanta and Columbia — were burned, and left largely in ruins. The poor whites for once in life found their poverty a blessing. The slaves for the most part watched the Yankees bring them freedom with stolid curiosity.

The Civil War left the United States where it began, divided and with hatred the worse, the North intoxicated by the profits of force, the South crushed and greatly impoverished, and the social problems everywhere unsettled. The capital savings of the south, that of a third of the population of the United States, in currency, bonds and stocks, had gone into the necessities of war. The livestock and equipment of farm, factory and railroads were swept away or worn out. The labor system was in chaos and the earning power of whites and blacks uncertain. For the North war-time production had under artificial stimuli, that is war spending and harder work, reduced financial losses as measured by taxes and debts, and for a few, profits were excessive. For the majority inflation meant a lower standard of living. For the nation as a whole the losses in national wealth and income were incalculable. Competent scholars have estimated the total money costs of the war at well over twenty billion dollars. It was an amount well over ten times liberal estimates of the total money value of the slaves to their owners, and takes no account of the heritage of death, desolation, the sufferings of the living and the social problems which remained the worse for civil war. It also fails to include the great mortality which prevailed for many years among the freedmen, "a laboring, landless, and homeless class," in Lincoln's words; "free from the old masters, but the slaves of society, turned loose, naked, hungry and destitute to the open sky," as one of their own leaders said. Nor does any estimate of the cost of the Civil War include the utterly demoralizing years of the rule of the Ku Klux Klan, embittering the races and retarding production of the necessities for living.

X. RECONSTRUCTION IN THE SOUTH DIRECTED BY REVENGE AND IDEALISM

CONGRESS REPUDIATES LINCOLN'S PLANS — The Civil War had given an impetus to the national shape of things, political and industrial; whether a blessing remained for future generations to learn. One sure asset was the emancipation of the slaves, and that was no small gain, and another the preservation of the Union, for it had become the greatest issue by the challenge of the South. In efforts to justify and glorify the heroism of the war and its great achievements historians have often been blind to the offsetting spiritual losses and tremendous costs. Ideals of social justice which had grown up since the Revolution gave way after the Civil War to *laissez faire* and selfish profiteering. Idealism, as it were, had spent itself in the great sacrifices over slavery.

Instead of the peace of justice and restoration of national good will which President Lincoln advocated, there followed ten years of military rule of the South, "the bottom rail on top," as the freedmen said. What the historians for a generation after the Civil War called the Reconstruction period, what a later one named the Tragic Era, was a fantastic political and social adventure, enthroning the black proletariat in government, marshalled by generals and northern carpetbaggers with the former white rulers hamstrung in public life. It was a peace, the combination of idealism and revenge, idealistic in form for the former slaves and punitive for the old ruling classes. It was a travesty on real reconstruction, having little to do with the needed social readjustments.

The system imposed upon the South did not work, but it did aggravate the problems produced by war, resulting in economic and social anarchy, and disillusionment. In 1877 when President Hayes withdrew the army from the South and allowed the whites to disfranchise the negroes and recover home rule, the Federal government recognized the futility of the course it had taken. The readjustments so necessary for negroes and whites were left to the southern states and a new era began.

ECONOMIC ISOLATION ADOPTED — In other ways the Civil War shaped the course of events which followed. The passions aroused by four years of bloodshed made rational peace measures impossible no matter who proposed them. Lincoln's plans for gradual racial adjustments in the South and his Secretary of the Treasury's equally well considered ones for monetary and tariff reform, made necessary by hasty Civil War legislation, miscarried. In their places: (1) a seemingly endless racial conflict came to prevail in the South, doubly serious because the conflicts over reconstruction drove an irremovable wedge between the whites, North and South, a barrier to satisfactory approaches to any national problems; (2) the inflationary greenbacks remained to become a perennial temptation for the discontented, producing a state of national confusion whenever money became an issue; (3) and the Civil War tariffs became the road to a large degree of national economic isolation, more significant than political isolation. As it happened, enormous resources, an industrial revolution, world wide, and a flood of low and ever lower income groups of immigrants concealed the maladjustments that were piling up in country and city life.

After the Civil War the nation really took the road to quick wealth by the rapid exploitation of its natural resources, hoping, of course, that it would benefit all. It was a process which could not work that way, however, for the barriers to hordes of immigrants were down. Unconsciously it paved the way to slum areas in the cities and the loss of world markets for the farmers of the Far West.

CLEVELAND BENEFITS FROM THE INDUSTRIAL REVOLUTION — In the industrial changes which followed the Civil War Cleveland had more than its full share, and benefited as few other cities did. The foundations had been laid in the 'fifties; the Civil War gave a great impetus to the expansion of these industries. A great waterway, railroads and some years later pipe lines, and, as a result, the ever increasing flow of coal from Ohio, iron ore from upper Michigan and oil from Pennsylvania gave form to the process of development. The waterway to Lake Superior turned the flow of iron ore to Cleveland, the building of the Atlantic and the Great Western (Erie) into Cleveland started oil toward the same center. The Erie Railroad entered the oil fields from the North, giving Cleveland an advantage over Pittsburgh, which it never lost. Iron and petroleum products dominated its manufacturing.

By 1868 the Board of Trade reported some fourteen rolling mills in and about Cleveland not to speak of the manufacturies of machinery of all kinds — stoves, castings, mouldings, bar iron, nails and spikes, iron for bridges and railroad equipment. With the introduction of the Bessemer process of making cheap steel, steel mills were added. But through it all the iron trade, in all its phases from ore in the mines to the finished product, remained highly competitive. At no time did one ore company or rolling mill dominate the field.

The opposite was the history of the petroleum business. One man, John D. Rockefeller, gave character to the development of the oil business in Cleveland. Whether it was as a younger partner in Andrews, Clark and Company, buried in the "company", or an equal partner in Rockefeller and Andrews, or Rockefeller, Andrews and Flagler, or the Standard Oil Company, John D. Rockefeller shaped the course. Competition melted away. Size, efficiency and railroad favors were together too much for rivals. Measured by years the process took time. As late as 1884 in Cleveland there were 86 refineries of varying sizes. One by one most of them accepted Rockefeller's terms, his price on their works or a share in the Standard Oil. If the former it was to be an unhappy choice, if the latter the road to undreamed of riches. It is significant as Orth in his *History of Cleveland* has written — "The older industries of making burr stones, pot and pearl ashes, of saleratus and of candle and lard oil" had yielded to industries that dealt with iron ore, coal, petroleum and clothing.

Year by year there came into Cleveland's business life organizations which have lived and grown through all the years which have followed. In 1866 the Sherwin Williams Company, the Grasselli Chemical Company, the Cleveland Cooperative Stove Company, and the Hugh Huntington Roofing Company; in 1867, Babcock and Wilcox was founded, followed the next year by Fries and Schuele, National Malleable and Steel Castings Company, and the H. H. Hackman leather company; in 1869, David Round and Son, Webb C. Ball and Lamson and Sessions, the Cleveland Directory Company, the Glidden Company and the Tinnerman Products Company.

LITTLE AFFECTED BY THE RECONSTRUCTION QUARRELS — What happened in the South under Reconstruction seemed to have little effect on Clevelanders. The former slave states were a remote region. They had not become the source of Cleveland's winter

fruits and vegetables. The last year of the War and those following were an era of rapid growth, founded on steel and oil, on commerce by rail and water. Under such conditions, with all the
opportunities for work and new business, the population grew
rapidly, increasing 100 per cent in ten years (1866-1876). (1866,
67,500; 1876, about 135,000). The majority of the population
was either foreign born or of foreign parentage, and these largely
of British or Germanic origin. Immigrants from South and
Southeastern Europe whether from the slav or romance countries,
were negligible. As it was, the New England element in Cleveland
had become distinctly a minority, what with the inflow of native
elements from neighboring states, other parts of Ohio, and the
foreign groups. And yet, the older, established families of the
professions, industry and business as well were still predominantly of the old Connecticut stock.

XI. THE SLOW RECOVERY IN CULTURAL LIFE

CLEVELAND GROWS LIKE TOPSY — At the close of the Civil War
Cleveland extended from East 55th Street (Old Willson) to
West 58th Street (formerly Waverly Street). In 1872 the village
of East Cleveland was annexed, extending from Willson Street
to a short distance beyond Doan Brook. The following year
Newburg became the "iron ward" of Cleveland, not a very
flattering epithet for an historic community. Both additions were
the result of popular votes, though not without sharp opposition
in both villages. East Cleveland brought into Cleveland a population well over 5,000, Newburg over 6,000. Cleveland was
growing as Topsy did, adding suburbs like cells, by Divine
plan, if any, certainly not by man's, an awkward whole, with
streets seldom joining.

Idealism in Cleveland had spent itself in the emancipation
issue. Only slowly did the cultural activities which marked
the 'fifties revive as the population elements gained leisure or
security, or both.

In 1876 Cleveland had six daily newspapers, two of them in the

German language — *The Herald*, the *Leader*, the *Evening News*, *Plain Dealer*, *Anzeiger*, and the *Waechter am Erie*; there were three Sunday newspapers — the *Sunday Morning Voice*, *Post* and *Times*. The *Post* and the *Times* had too fragile a hold on life to last long. Like some other weeklies they were more ambitious for regularity than their incomes warranted. Several weekly and monthly publications were for special groups — national, religious, or occupational. The German population alone had besides the two dailies, two tri-weekly, four weekly, and three monthly publications.

THE BIG THREE NEWSPAPER EDITORS — The newspapers had not changed greatly, their editors still nagging one another for the benefit of their readers, though not quite so vitriolic as in the 'forties and 'fifties. Still they belonged to the class of journalists of the old school. William W. Armstrong had come to Cleveland in 1865 from Tiffin, Ohio, to revive the moribund *Plain Dealer*. For the remainder of this period Armstrong, George A. Benedict of the *Herald* and Edwin Cowles of the *Leader* were the big three of Cleveland journalism. Cowles' chief editorial phobias were negro slavery and the Catholics, the latter because of his fear that the Pope was going to take over the United States. Cowles has been compared to Horace Greeley. "His tremendous energy, his dauntless will, his relentless dogmatism and unchanging attachments were all dominated by an eccentric personality that was at once powerful and tender," a description which would have fitted either journalist.[16]

The editors of the *Leader* and the *Herald*, both Republican partisans, waged a continuous verbal battle. Cowles could think the Democratic editor of the *Plain Dealer* a gentleman without admiring his political choice; he could not say as much for Benedict or any of his associates of the *Leader*. The *Leader* was a morning paper, the others evening. In 1861 it began to

[16] Orth, I, 516.

71

offer also an afternoon edition, embittering the factional strife among the Republicans. From 1868 the afternoon edition became the *Evening News*. So far in Cleveland History three newspaper men had left the stamp of their personality on their times —Gray of the *Plain Dealer*, Harris of the *Herald*, and Cowles of the *Leader*. And this means in cultural things as well as in their business success.

BRAINARD'S MUSICAL WORLD — From the point of view of cultural influence *Brainard's Musical World*, or the *Western Musical World*, as it sometimes chose to be called, started in 1864, was an important force. It was published by the house of S. Brainard and Sons, publishers and retailers of musical books, sheets, and whatever would advance the cause of music and yield a profit to the firm. Its business included musical instruments, and the members of the firm promoted concerts and other musical events. Brainard's Hall, the Melodeon, over their store, was for the most of this period a musical center, sharing the honors with the Academy of Music and after 1867 with Case Hall. One of the sons edited the *World*, which started off in 1864 with an edition of 2,000 copies; in 1871 the issue was 25,000, eminently successful. It called itself a "journal of music, art and literature," and it might have added the drama, for its columns carried the news of the theaters. The introductory article said the *World* would be devoted to the cause of "Music and Fine Arts in the Great West." It gave its readers new, informal opinions and extensive articles in its several fields and with each issue a reprint from three to six pieces of music.

Various other organizations represented the cause of music which was taking on more substantial forms after the Civil War. In 1871 the Cleveland Conservatory of Music was started with William Heydler at the head, announcing each year courses in music for Cleveland youth. In 1874 it occupied the upper rooms in architect Heard's "magnificent stone building," Heard's Block at Sheriff and Euclid. In the same year Alfred Arthur started a School of Music, the beginnings of one that was to find a permanent place in the Cleveland educational system. In the public and private schools, teachers of music added to the forces cultivating the subject, as did the several regular choral organizations. There was the Philharmonic Society, now many years old, and the Mendelssohn Choral Society, and after 1873, Alfred Arthur's Vocal Society. And there were the Gesaengverein and other less successful societies with a short lived tenure. But these were the days of the promotion of choral organizations.

A NATIONAL MUSICAL FESTIVAL IN CLEVELAND—The number of musical events during the years following the Civil War was not impressive. A foreign opera company for a fortnight, an occasional concert by the Cleveland Harmonic Society, and perhaps a few evenings of music by Theodore Thomas' Orchestra were the usual season's record. Ole Bull continued his annual visits to Cleveland, as before the Civil War. In 1873, the combination of the great artists Anton Rubinstein and Wieniawski with Theodore Thomas and his orchestra came to Cleveland bringing what the newspapers called the best musical talent ever, a season's climax. However, the great musical event in Cleveland for the decade following the War was the Nineteenth National Saengerfest of June, 1874. (Saengerfests had met in Cleveland in 1854 and 1859). The Saengerfest was a national union of German Singing societies, holding annual musical festivals.

For the occasion in Cleveland a Gesaengverein Hall was constructed on the property of Horace P. Weddell, on Euclid Avenue, a short distance west of Case Avenue. For the time it was a mammoth hall, seating some ten thousand.[17] Carl Bergmann was the conductor. His Philharmonic Orchestra of New York and Madame Pauline Lucca, the Prussian *prima donna*, were the

17 No two of the newspapers of the day agree on the exact location. I have followed the *Waechter am Erie*, May 11, 1874, checked by locating the Weddell property in the records of the County recorder.

chief features of the occasion. *Brainard's Musical World* published the program in full, and listed seventy-four German Societies of the United States that were expecting to attend. The railroads gave half-fare rates and the lake steamers special concessions. The several choral societies of Cleveland and the pupils of the public schools participated in the program, N. Coe Stewart, director of music in the schools, their conductor. For the day in which the pupils participated the schools were closed, and what a day. The whole city seemed to be participating, the streets and business houses were decorated, the hall crowded to capacity. The Saengerfest of 1874 is ample proof that Cleveland had accepted its German citizens as its own, and of its musical appreciation as well.

In August, 1902, the *Wachter und Anzeiger* published a golden jubilee number. It presented the great cultural influence of the Germans in Cleveland over fifty years, and that influence was most notable in the development of music.

JOHN ELLSLER PUTS THE DRAMA ON THE MAP — The history of the drama in Cleveland from 1855 to 1877, or, in fact, until 1878 (when he lost control of the Euclid Avenue Opera House) was almost entirely the record of the activities of John A. Ellsler, lessee and manager of the Academy of Music and for a brief time of the Opera House. In all his activities his wife, Effie, and his daughters, Anna and Effie (Mrs. Weston) were a part, particularly on the stage. His grand-daughter, Miss Virginia Ellsler, has recently given the Society, among many relics of her Aunt Effie, a copy of the Stage Memories of John A. Ellsler, an invaluable record of his career on the stage and of his Cleveland days. (Historical Society's Manuscripts, No. 3025. Edited by Effie Ellsler Weston).

Ellsler maintained a stock company, partly, of course, a family affair, but also containing other regular members and visiting stars on occasion. He took them to neighboring cities in off seasons or when opportunities offered in order to support his theater. For a while after 1871 he also managed the Pittsburgh Opera House. In 1875 he was operating the Pittsburgh Opera House, the Academy of Music and the new Euclid Avenue Opera House in Cleveland. His stock companies alternated between Pittsburgh and Cleveland, enriching the dramatic talent available in both cities during a season. Of his experience he wrote: "Financially, the seasons in Pittsburgh were in advance of those in Cleveland, the public being more of an amusement loving community, and lavish in their disbursements of money, of which there always seemed to be an abundance. Among the wealthiest, the purse strings were ever open. Self-made men, familiar with the ups and downs of life in its different phases, were ready with their hands outstretched to help the one in the valley of despond. I speak from experience."[18]

THE EUCLID AVENUE OPERA HOUSE — By 1873 the Academy of Music no longer adequately served the needs of a manager as ambitious and energetic as John Ellsler. It was old, outmoded and too small for his plans. Associated with several local friends, he organized a stock company. Sam Briggs, known to the Historical Society circles of the time, was Secretary of the Company. Architect Heard planned for them a magnificent house, one that according to newspaper accounts, would have been noticeable upon a central park in some old European city, with an elaborate stone front, marble foyers and interior decorations befitting the remainder of the structure. But misfortune awaited their grandiose scheme. Ellsler mentions the "Panic of 1873" as the first. But they had made their house face Sheriff Street, counting on the city council to widen the street as a thoroughfare, a project like so many others in Cleveland to die a still death. Ellsler staked his all, when his associates found themselves unable to go along with their subscriptions. It was completed and opened September 6, 1875, with Bronson Howard's "Saratoga" or "Pistols for

[18] Mss. no. 3025, p. 152.

Seven," with the Ellsler family in the cast and eighteen others, including Lewis Davenport and Fannie Morant, a satire on the vanities and follies of life at Saratoga.

The famous actor, Edward A. Sothern, who visited Cleveland in May, 1876, playing in "Our American Cousins," called the Opera House "the most perfect theater in America or England." However, the promise of a new day for the drama in Cleveland was clouded by the impending disaster which the courageous manager had to face. Pittsburgh was the family's remaining hope. There was some glory in the record, nevertheless. Ellsler could write in his Memories: "In Cleveland we succeeded in presenting all the prominent stars then travelling in any branch of the theatrical profession. Every star, male or female. Every Opera Company, foreign or domestic, all Burlesques or Opera Bouffe Companies, all the pantomine troupes, every Comedian and Tragedian that travelled from 1855 to 1873, they all walked the boards of the old Academy of Music while under my management."[19] In his list of the stars whom he brought to Cleveland are the names of Edwin Forrest, Charlotte Cushman, Charlotte Thompson, Joseph Proctor, Charles Keen, Frank Mayo, John McCullough, Joseph Jefferson, Edward A. Sothern, Lawrence Barrett and Edwin Adams, an honorable roll for a city which had only recently been on the untravelled frontier of the theater.

Ellsler's stock companies were excellent dramatic schools of the day, for Cleveland all there was. In 1872 he brought on a new flock of actors from Boston and New York. One of his pupils, Clara Morris, (nee Clara Morrison) became in later years a frequent star visitor. In 1867 "Little Effie Ellsler" made her first Cleveland appearance in *Ten Nights in a Bar Room*. Ellsler's promotional activities included music and lecturers in his programs at the Academy of Music. Foreign Opera companies were a regular feature of annual entertainment.

19 Mss. no. 3025, Memories, p. 116.

THE SLOW RECOVERY IN CULTURAL LIFE

After giving Ellsler's share in the cultural life, the net result may be summed up from an editorial in the *Cleveland Leader*, January 6, 1874. "The great lights of the dramatic stage seldom put in an appearance at Cleveland, and why: because no manager can afford to bring them here unless it is for the luxury of losing money. In opera we have occasionally a fraction of a company . . . We have an average of one public entertainment a week other than the theater . . . If Cleveland people had the enterprise they have credit for, Case Hall, Brainard's Opera House, and Garrett's Hall would be filled with audiences every night. We should have an art gallery where pictures and statues from master hands would revolutionize our ideas. We should have a public library of 100,000 volumes. Then, too, our churches are not attended as they should be."

Five years earlier Cowles had complained that "one of the most astonishing features of the City of Cleveland is the immense disparity between the literary and commercial interests of the city." [20] Cleveland's cultural interests came, it seems, by flashes, when Ellsler brought a star or the German citizens a Gesaengerfest. The population as a whole was still under the shadow of the Civil War, Reconstruction, and the lure of business opportunities.

In ante-bellum days Clevelanders took their culture seriously, relying chiefly on the church, the newspaper and public lectures. It is difficult to measure the influence of editors and ministers, and for that matter the lecturers, the dramatists or the musicians. The temptation is to try to do so by the quantity method. Of course, it may not be a sequence — the more lecturers there are the more culture there will be. But anyway, the Civil War saw the decline in the public lecture in Cleveland. The series offered by the Cleveland Library Association and the Young Men's Christian Association almost died out, an unhappy period for

20 Cleveland Leader, October 19, 1869.

the annual crop of eastern and foreign lecturers. Only an occasional star in the field could command audiences. One can be sure that Artemus Ward with his lecture "Among the Mormons" or the other, "Babes in the Woods," with not a word about the babes; P. T. Barnum on "The Art of Money Getting" or "Success in Life;" Mark Twain, "A Vandal Abroad" and Bret Hart, "The Argonauts of 1849" had their full houses. The usual lecturers announced in the newspapers were second raters; occasionally there was a visit by a popular orator of the day like Wendell Phillips or Horace Greeley whose idiosyncracies always brought out an audience filled with curiosity.

THE PORTRAIT PAINTERS — The revival in art after the Civil War seemed from the records to be slower than that of the other members of the fine arts group — music and drama. Especially does this seem to be the case, if one depends on newspaper sources. Perhaps the artists were less fortunate in their publicity. Three, however, seemed to make up for the apparent backwardness of the profession as a whole — Allen Smith, Caroline L. Ransom and Archibald M. Willard. Allen Smith, by now the dean of Cleveland artists, was still going strong. His portrait of Dr. Jared P. Kirtland should for obvious reasons, if it is available, be one of the prized possessions of the Cleveland Museum of Natural History, and that of Benjamin Rouse eventually come to the Historical Society. In 1866 Congress allowed Miss Ransom $1,000 for her portrait of Joshua Giddings, and nine years later $15,000 for one of General Thomas, so the Cleveland newspapers reported, both to be placed in the Capitol building. Either the congressional appraisal of the artist's merits or of those of the national heroes had grown markedly. When it is remembered that the purchasing value of the dollar of that time would be four or five times what it is seventy-five years later Miss Ransom's prices became something of an occasion for envy by modern artists. Perhaps the readers will find several conclusions to be drawn from the tale.

Miss Ransom was a familiar figure in Washington, spending several seasons in the capital painting portraits of the great and the near great. The Historical Society possesses five examples of her work in Cleveland, including a portrait of Colonel Charles Whittlesey, its first president, and a full length portrait in uniform of President James A. Garfield at "Lawnfield," the Garfield home in Mentor.

The photographic establishment of J. F. Ryder on Superior Street was described in the newspapers of the 'sixties and 'seventies as an Art Gallery with engravings, oils, and crayons on the walls, "an art store and photograph gallery combined." Ryder, in his Recollections," Voigtlander and I," says it had a large exhibition window in front, approached by a vestibule entrance through graceful double columns where was always a fine exhibit of interesting pictures. In the rear was also a special exhibition room. The exhibition of contemporary artists gave the place a May Show air. For the most part the artists were selling reproductions of old masters. One artist, encouraged by Ryder, achieved an enviable national reputation. In December, 1875, the *Cleveland Leader* reported two paintings by A. M. Willard — the "Roman Prisoner" and "Venus." They were sold to a local dentist for $1500, so the editor reported in his column. We presume he had secret sources of information. The former was exhibited for a time in the New York Academy of Design.

ARCHIBALD M. WILLARD, FROM WAGON PAINTER TO FUN MAKER—
Born in Bedford, Ohio, after serving through the Civil War, Willard settled in Wellington, Ohio, as a painter in the shop of a local wagon maker. He was soon decorating his employer's wagons and circus chariots with gaudy animals and woodland scenes. It is evident that he was possessed of a strong sense of humor. He learned to paint in oil on canvas, and in the early 'seventies painted for his employer's daughter "Pluck Number One." Other humorous pictures followed. He took his work to

J. F. Ryder in Cleveland who helped him market it in the form of photographs and colored chromos. His relations with Ryder must have given him professional independence. For several months, in 1873 he studied art in New York City with J. O. Eaton, and shortly after this adventure he moved to Cleveland. In the meantime other humorous pictures had come from his brush — "Pluck Number Two," "The Awkward Squad" and "Deacon Jones' Experience," for example, for which Ryder was finding a market in the form of chromos, at $5.00 each. Ryder in his Recollections tells that he was afraid Deacon Jones' Experience would offend the pious and that he paid Bret Harte two hundred dollars to write an inoffensive poem on the subject. This he circulated with the chromos.[21]

EVOLUTION OF THE "SPIRIT OF '76" — Among Willard's humorous paintings was one which he called "The Fourth of July Musicians" or "Yankee Doodle," a representation of a Fourth of July celebration in a country village. Willard's father was an old drummer in the picture. Whether it was an impulse to represent his dying father in a serious vein or a sense of timeliness in the opportunity offered by the approaching Centennial in Philadelphia, he turned to drawing sketches for a large, patriotic painting. One of his crayon sketches representing a further stage in the development of his ideas has been preserved in the Herrick Memorial Library in Wellington, along with the humorous "Yankee Doodle." The scene has begun to take on a martial air, but much of the later conception is still lacking.

On March 28, 1876, the *Cleveland Leader* announced that "a painting by A. M. Willard of this city was yesterday placed on exhibition in Ryder's window. The canvas is intended for the Centennial and is called 'Yankee Doodle.' The painting illustrates the spirit of old '76." The following day the editor gave a

---

21 The Historical Society has these humorous paintings on permanent exhibition in the Museum.

long, half column, description of the picture. One sentence is significant. "At their feet is a dismantled cannon on the ruins of which a dead soldier lies, his peaceful sleep in sad contrast to the motion and action all about him." The *Cleveland Herald's* description still another day later says of the bottom of the picture — "In the foreground at one side lies a fallen soldier and a crippled artillery carriage." The size of the whole is not remarked as particularly impressive. Three points are significant — dead soldier, broken cannon, unimpressive size. Add to this the statement of Henry K. Devereux who had posed as the drummer boy that Willard's studio was a small room on the fourth floor of a building at Hickox Alley and Euclid Street (the site of the Central National Bank in 1945). A few weeks later, May 25, a correspondent for the *Cleveland Plain Dealer* at the Centennial in Philadelphia reported upon it. On two points it is still the same picture — as to size and broken cannon. The dead soldier, however, has been resurrected. "The dying soldier is lifting his weak hand to once more wave his cap, opening his lips for one more weak hurrah."

Before sending the picture to Philadelphia Willard had responded to criticism, enlarged his conception, by giving movement to the entire picture. The soldier was brought into the "spirit of '76." Willard visited the Centennial Exposition in the Fall and apparently from the fragmentary records available painted two new versions during the following months or years. On February 14, 1877, James F. Ryder presented one, a large one, the largest known, 8 by 13 feet, to the Cleveland Grays, which is supposed to have been destroyed in a fire some years later. A second one, a grand, colorful version, 8 by 10 feet, was at some time in the late 'seventies, sent to the Cocharan Art Gallery in Washington. The one that had been at the Centennial travelled in the meantime to Boston, to San Francisco, and back to Boston to a place in Old South Church. Here it remained for several years, in time to be returned to Cleveland to come to rest in Ryder's galleries until the Western

Reserve Historical Society acquired it from the owner of the galleries after Ryder's death.

At this point in history, 1880, General John H. Devereux appears, a Cleveland engineer, railway executive and philanthropist. His son was the drummer boy. General Devereux wanted such a memorial for the family home town of Marblehead, Mass., and proposed to purchase the Cocharan Art Gallery copy. Mrs. Henry K. Devereux has in recent years told Mr. Cathcart the story. It seems that her father-in-law did not like the sprawling, broken cannon, conspicuous as it was in the Centennial painting.[22] In the Cocharan version the offensive broken cannon had disappeared entirely from the one Devereux purchased except for a part of a wheel. There are other refinements.

In 1880 General Devereux presented it to the town of Marblehead to be exhibited in Abbott Hall. And that this was not the same or a revised edition of an earlier painting is made emphatic by a statement of Willard's son, Byron, that his father painted the Marblehead picture in a large vacant room in the City Hall's quarters in the Case Block.[23] The Cleveland City Directories confirm his statement by locating the artist's studio in the City Hall for many years following 1876.[24] If Willard, as Devereux says, had a studio in a building at Hickox Alley and Euclid Street it was a temporary arrangement. In 1926 the drummer boy, grown man, privately printed a monograph on the "Spirit of '76." His abridged account has misled students of the subject.

The evolution did not end here. In 1892 the selectmen of Marblehead returned the painting to Cleveland for Willard to repair. Byron Willard later said that his father had not been

22 Mrs. King Daywalt, curator of the Society's Museum was also present when Mrs. Devereux told her story.

23 Byron Willard was for many years a civil engineer in Shaker Heights.

24 The Directory of 1875-1876 gives a room, 205 Superior, as the location of Willard's studio, that of 1876-1877, the City Hall.

content with a repairing job but had made several alterations, some of which he described.[25] The changes were so numerous that one may easily come to believe a new picture took the place of the one sent for repair. In that case the one in need of repairs became one of Willard's discards. Only expert, technical studies of the present painting in Marblehead, perhaps with infra-red, will establish the full history of the "Spirit of '76." The repainted picture, that is, the second Abbott Hall replica, reverts in many details to the form of the more primitive painting which is now in the Western Reserve Historical Society. Even the broken cannon reappears, though somewhat softened and truncated.

For historical purposes the evolution was now complete. A version in the Cleveland City Hall, painted by Willard under a commission from Mayor Newton D. Baker, in 1912, and another by Willard for his friend, the Reverend W. E. Barton, in 1916, and which is now in the Herrick Library in Wellington, add nothing to the development of this remarkable conception.

There are, it should be said, seven "originals" which have had a part in this evolutionary process. The Western Reserve Historical Society has the one that made history in 1876. It rested in the rear of James F. Ryder's Art Gallery, a discard of the author, through the remainder of Ryder's life, passed through the hands of several successors, and was finally sold to Mr. Cathcart, Director of the Historical Society, by A. L. Bowersox, who had come into the possession of Ryder's establishment with its accumulated treasures. Mr. Cathcart rested his case for having the one sent to Philadelphia in 1876 on the testimony of Bowersox, Mrs. Devereux and Mrs. Connelly, Willard's daughter. The examination of the technical development in the successive "originals" and fragmentary newspaper items seem even more convincing. Certainly there were no exact copies. The artist seemed

25 Western Reserve Historical Society, Mss. 2174.

indisposed to copy his own works. Visitors to the Historical Society's Museum will find photographs of the several versions of "The Spirit of '76" on exhibition, showing the changes in its successive stages.[26]

For the history of art in Cleveland another event of the centennial year was of greater promise for things to come than the painting by Willard of the "Spirit of '76." That was the formation of an art club, meeting regularly on Monday nights, room open every evening, at least, such was the hope, a combination of a club and a teaching center for those not practised in the art. Willard was the president, and the club room was in the City Hall, perhaps in Willard's studio. In the following year a number of Clevelanders interested in art attempted to organize an Academy of Fine Arts. A board of trustees was created, of which body Willard was again one. That he was becoming a factor in the development of art in his new environment seems certain. The happenings at the end of this third period in Cleveland history foreshadowed a new era for the local artists.

A HISTORICAL SOCIETY, TOO — In spite of the all-pervasive nature of the racial problems during the Civil War and Reconstruction, perhaps because they had deepened an interest in the course of events, several Clevelanders had turned to the history of their own region. For many years John Barr and Colonel Whittlesey had been gathering material and writing on Cleveland history, quite independent of one another. In 1846 John Barr, attorney, county sheriff, judge, successively, had written a short history of Cleveland. At this time and later he gathered a large collection of surveyor's notes, and pioneers' reminiscences, invaluable records all. The Society has two bound volumes of the field notes of the surveyors sent out by the Connecticut Land Company, which came from attorney John Barr.

26 In this history of the "Spirit of '76" I am under obligation for cordial cooperation of Karl O. Townsend of Wellington, Ohio, and William F. Bragdon, Town Clerk of Marblehead, Massachusetts, Henry S. Francis of the Cleveland Art Museum, and Henry Hunt Clark of the Cleveland School of Art.

THE SLOW RECOVERY IN CULTURAL LIFE

From the time he arrived in Cleveland in the 'thirties, Charles Whittlesey had also been an indefatigable writer in the fields of archeology, economic geography and history. His biographer lists 191 books and pamphlets which he published during his lifetime, besides the innumerable articles published in newspapers and scientific serials. His manuscript field notes and diaries in the Historical Society are additional evidence of his work. A bachelor until fairly late in life, research in field and in study was his passion. He was as versatile in his work as was his great contemporary, Dr. Jared P. Kirtland, a friend, and at times a co-worker. Whittlesey's paper written for the Tallmadge semi-centennial (in 1857) constitutes one of the best accounts of log cabin days, being really personal reminiscences.

Whittlesey's greatest published work was a volume on the "Early History of Cleveland." It was weighted heavily with archaeological information and the very early record of the region. Sections on the Pre-Adamites, Pre-Historic Inhabitants, the Red Man, Early Explorers and the Moravians and the First Whites consumed nearly one-third of the volume, the remaining two-thirds were largely reprints of the notes and journals of the surveyors for the Connecticut Land Company and sketches of the pioneers of the Western Reserve, source material nearly all. It formed the author's conception of the history of the Cleveland region before the War of 1812. In the preface he says, "I am more ambitious to preserve history than to write it." "Early Cleveland" represented just that ideal. He would have regarded the work of his last twenty years of life as the climax of his career, the founding and early development of the Historical Society — a place primarily for the preservation of the materials of history in library and museum.

THE BEGINNINGS — The story of the origin and early history of the Historical Society is part of the History of the Cleveland Library Association, Case Library of later years. Early in 1867 the Association moved into the Case Hall at Wood (East Third) and Superior, Leonard Case having given it the use of three rooms. Among the trustees of the Association were two who were very much interested in history, Charles Candee Baldwin and Charles Whittlesey. M. B. Scott was the president. He and Joseph Perkins, John Barr, Alfred Goodman and H. A. Smith were in sympathy with Baldwin and Whittlesey and parties to the project to do something about the rather dormant interest in history at the time. In May, 1867, this group acting through the Library Association decided to establish not one but two specialized departments — a historical and a scientific department, drawing Dr. Kirtland and others into their movement.

A few days later (June 5, 1867) the organization of the historical department was completed with Whittlesey as President. The President of the Library Association, M. B. Scott, became Vice President of the Department. The board of six curators with the President, Treasurer, and Chairman of the Library Committee as ex-officio members had some trouble in naming their child. They thought of it as the Historical Department of the Cleveland Library Association. That was its actual legal status. As yet, it had no charter to give it an independent existence. In the By-Laws adopted on June 5, the name in its later form, the Western Reserve Historical Society, first appeared on the record, though for many years the Society's official stationery used a longer title . . . The Western Reserve and Northern Ohio Historical Society. The new organization announced its purpose "to discover, procure and preserve whatever relates to the history, biography, genealogy, antiquities and statistics connected with the City of Cleveland and the Western Reserve." And to make sure that all interests of Cleveland would come within its field, they added "and generally what relates to the History of Ohio and the Great West," a comprehensive order. The officers secured quarters on the third floor of the Society for Savings' new building at the northeast corner of the Public Square, for a museum and library of history, all in one long room. For several years the Library Association paid the rent and the Bank provided the heat.

THE SLOW RECOVERY IN CULTURAL LIFE

THE KIRTLAND SOCIETY OF NATURAL SCIENCE — Apparently the Academy of Natural Science, a casualty of the Civil War, came to a momentary life in the spring of 1867. The newspapers announced a meeting at which officers were chosen, President Dr. Kirtland, and Vice Presidents, Charles Whittlesey, Rufus K. Winslow and Captain B. A. Stannard, the last two, Arkites. It would seem that Kirtland and Whittlesey were preparing the way to draw the organization into a part in the new movement in the Library Association. There is no record of another meeting of the scientific group for two years. In 1869 it was reorganized as the Kirtland Society of Natural Science and the following year took its place as a department of the Cleveland Library Association, apparently having difficulty in giving up its former complete independence. Several years later (1876) the Society opened a Natural History Museum in Case Hall, adjacent to the Library and the lecture hall which gave the building its name. Case Hall was projected by William Case as a center for such purposes, planned with Faneuil Hall, Boston, as a civic and architectural model in mind. In developing his plan he visited Boston. It was not completed until after his death. Located on Superior Street, just west of Third Street, adjacent to the Federal Post Office, Architect, C. H. Heard.

In the Minute Book of the Historical Society is an agreement between the Library Association, the Historical Society and the Kirtland Society providing for reciprocal privileges of members, for admission at one another's lectures, exhibitions, libraries and for the exchange of specimens, recognizing at the same time the complete autonomy of each. It is also a matter of record that the Library Association transferred to the Historical Society its works on local history.

The parent of these new institutions, the Cleveland Library Association, was clearly on the way to a large place in the intellectual life of Clevelanders. In 1870 Leonard Case gave it an endowment fund of $25,000 and a perpetual lease of the rooms on the second floor of the Case Hall. Six years later he gave the Association the building, valued at $300,000.

A PUBLIC LIBRARY — In the late 'sixties cultural interests had seemed to take on new vigor — what with the Cleveland Library Association, the Western Reserve Historical Society and the Kirtland Society of Natural Science. Nor was that the end of the revived intellectual interests. Just after the Civil War the State of Ohio had authorized communities to tax their property for library purposes. In 1869 the Cleveland Board of Education established such a library, a free circulating library, supported by one-tenth of a mill tax. Some years later its name became the Cleveland Public Library, still under the auspices of the Board of Education.

It was the Cleveland Public School Library, a part of the educational system under the auspices of the Board of Education. At the time Edwin R. Perkins was President of the Board, L. M. Oviatt the first librarian. For a few years it was located on Superior, west of Seneca, (Third). In 1875 it moved into unoccupied quarters of the City Hall, gravitating as other institutions had to this new center of the life of Cleveland, eastward as did everything else.

THE FLIGHT TO THE SUBURBS BEGINS — Two moves in the mid-seventies, one a business house and the other a family residence, showed the course of development upon which Cleveland had entered. After the Chicago fire of 1871, the Cobb brothers, by now in Cleveland known as Cobb, Andrews and Co., left Chicago, concentrating their business in Cleveland. While keeping their place on lower Superior, they opened a new store on Euclid Avenue, just east of the Public Square. (A location now occupied by Grant Co.) A rather flamboyant announcement in the newspapers told the story. "The opening by Messrs. Cobb, Andrews and Company of their new and magnificent Euclid Avenue establishment is an important event, not only

The Old City Hall. The Case Building, completed in 1875, leased by the City in 1875 — Architect, C. W. Heard.

An Afternoon in Euclid Street in the 'Seventies. From the Euclid Street Presbyterian Church at Brownell (East 14th) to the Euclid Street Baptist Church at Huntington Street (East 18th) — From a drawing by A. M. Willard — A Spirited Scene.

A view from the Reservoir Walk. On Franklin Street, near Franklin Circle, Overlooking the Harbor.

in the history of that old, well known firm, but also of the city, for that bookselling house came into existence almost as soon as Cleveland became a city, has grown with its growth and prospered with its prosperity. Cincinnati, Chicago or St. Louis cannot match it."[27] But it meant more. It spelled the doom of the glory of Euclid Avenue as one of the most beautiful residence streets in America.

Of similar import for Cleveland was the move of William J. Gordon, the leading merchant of the day, from his old home on north Water Street (West Ninth) to a beautiful park-like place at the mouth of Doan Brook, promise of things to come. Gordon's residence was still near the lake shore, with a magnificent outlook, but in itself a change of seat that marked the passing of the lake shore of Cleveland as a residence area, the doom of Lake Street and its approaches as the choice residence region it had long been. The mills and the railroads had taken over the city's outlook upon the magnificent gift nature had bestowed upon it.

XII. THE END OF ANOTHER ERA

THE SHAPE OF IMPENDING CHANGES—In more ways than one the passing of 1876 and the coming of 1877 marked the end of another period of national history. The shadow of Civil War and Reconstruction which had clouded the lives of a generation was clearing. In the election of 1876 the voters had registered dissatisfaction with the radical measures of reconstruction, whether they voted for Tilden or Hayes. Both were publically committed to a change in the national course. President Hayes' inauguration brought an end to military rule at the South, leaving reconstruction to the good will of the inhabitants therein. It was fitting that the changing feelings could be expressed and given a boost by the Centennial in Philadelphia. By 1877 the worst of the post civil war panic that began in 1873 was over. Cleveland had not

27 W. R. H. S. Mss. 3010.

suffered as many other parts of the country had; its development had been retarded only.

An era of consolidation of industry and transportation on a large scale had begun. The formation of the Standard Oil Company (1870) and the Lake Shore and Michigan Southern Railroad (1869), two Ohio corporations (offices in Cleveland), were signs of the changes coming everywhere. It was by such means corporations would meet the declining prices. Farmers would find it more difficult, and that would be the national and state political problem of the next decades. Two natives of the Western Reserve, Thomas A. Edison and Charles F. Brush, the latter of Cleveland, pointed the course that American History was to take. In his little workshop Brush had just invented a practical dynamo for producing electricity, and was on the eve of its successful use in an arc-light (1878). Edison would the following year produce the incandescent light. Alexander Graham Bell had only recently (1876) secured a patent for the first telephone. The electric motor was in the offing to produce a revolution in the application of electric power to man's activities. Since 1868 the Cleveland Rolling Mill Company of which Henry Chisholm was general manager had been applying the Bessemer process to the production of steel, making it cheap enough for a great variety of new uses. In order to insure an adequate supply of coal for Cleveland its capitalists had recently built the Massillon and Cleveland Railroad and the Lake Shore and Tuscarawas Valley Railroad, both reaching to the coal fields of the South. The impending change to the use of low priced steel, oil, electric light and power would transform the industrial parts of America. In this all Clevelanders would advantage. The Forest City was now clearly the oil capital of the United States, the inland ship building center and the distributing point for iron ore and coal. In 1873 the *Cleveland Leader* reported that the iron manufacturers alone employed 5000 men, oil refining 1600 more. And all this and more in one generation.

THE END OF ANOTHER ERA

One is tempted to end on a high note of progress and promise. But there is a dark and a light side to every cloud. One who reads the newspapers of the 'seventies knows that Cleveland by now had its unsanitary shanties, shacks and delapidated houses. The publicity the *Cleveland Leader* through July, August and September, 1873, gave "the foul slums, filthy yards and other pestilence — breeding places" was in itself an encouraging sign and a test for the coming years. The Mayor of Philadelphia once said that Philadelphia "unlike most cities has two rivers, and unlike most cities makes use of neither." Cleveland had a river and a lake, but the community as a whole ignored them. Aside from their use for navigation purposes, inadequate as they were, they were coming chiefly to be parts of a sewer system. The editor of the *Cleveland Leader* rejoiced that there was now a City Hall (he did not say that it was, as it always had been, in a rented building), an Opera House (did he know that it was near bankruptcy?), and a Break Water (meagre piers at the mouth of the Cuyahoga).

To make life more worth while there were more substantial things — the beginnings of a large variety of cultural agencies that mark a civilized community. In spite of the efforts of a few really able men and women who struggled to make Cleveland a better place for themselves and their children, it was far behind the older cities of the Atlantic coast, and those of the old world as a center of the fine arts, museums and educational facilities. It still bore the marks of the frontier, of a hasty and awkward growth.